58 Green Street

Christine King

Copyright © Christine King 2019

First Published in 2019 by
Level Heading

All rights reserved. Without limiting the rights under copyright reserved above, no part of this publication may be reproduced, stored in or introduced into a retrieval system, or transmitted, in any form or by any means (electronic, mechanical, photocopying, recording or otherwise), without the prior written permission of the copyright owner.

ISBN: 978-0-6481726-5-9

Cover photo by Christine King

A catalogue record for this book is available from the National Library of Australia

Design and layout by Level Heading – levelheading.com

Level Heading

Acknowledgements

Thanks to those who read the manuscript and gave honest feedback; Kenneth, Jack, Brian, Dianne, Joab.

The Castlemaine Word Mine group (Ann, Sally, Tricia, Val, Rosemary, Jean) was a huge help as we gathered every week, exchanging parts of our manuscripts, giving suggestions and encouragement.

When writing is something you love, that's the easy part, but it isn't the end. So thank you to Bernie for navigating me through all the other things that need doing in order to get to this stage.

58 Green Street has taken ten years to write, so thank you to anyone who has had to listen to me talking incessantly about "the book" that kept not happening!

And in case P. A. O' Reilly, author of *The Fine Colour of Rust*, ever reads this: as I read that book I realised why my book hadn't been working up till that point – I wasn't writing the way I talk. After reading that book the whole manuscript went through a radical change.

Contents

Part One

All the Fuss	9
Laugh at It	19
58 Green Street	25
Next Thing I Knew (1, 2)	42
Electroencephalogram	50
For Sale	59
Epileptic Interference	64
Jesus, Mary and Joseph	70
Taking Leave of My Senses	77
Attention All Visitors	88
Temporal Lobe Lesionectomy	97
Status	107
Buddha, Dharma, Sangha	113

Part Two

The times they are a-changin'	121
Generation Gap	128
Moshing to the Metal	135
Get a Real Job	143
Er …	150
First Time for Everything	156
We Don't Need You	164
Next Thing I Knew (3, 4, 5 & 6)	168
Not till You're Eighteen	180
Last Post	186
The times they are a-changin', again	195
Epilogue	203
Credits	205

Part One

All the Fuss

I used to put Finn over my shoulder after he'd had a feed and pat him on the back so he'd burp. Someone who's into baby-talk might call that a 'burpie'. Thankfully, today I've been educated. I know what a 'burpie' really is and its correct spelling as well.

"You stand up straight, jump with your hands above your head, bring yourself down to the ground and do one push up," my son tells me. I decide not to join in. After doing all that he brings himself back up to a standing position with complete ease, a smart little jump at the end of it. This is one *burpee*. "You do as many of those as you can until you think you can't keep going," he tells me. "Then you do one more."

"I'm impressed." I am. Not just with the exercise but the attitude too.

He owns a pair of push-up bars that look like huge door handles. This gives a person more height, in much the same way as a Pilate's ball makes sit-ups more effective. He owns one of them as well. He's got several weight stations for sit-ups and bench-presses, as well as dumbbells for biceps, triceps and pecs, a boxing bag, and a tyre to do step-ups on. He's given up smoking, has muscles on his muscles, tattoos, and grows an excellent beard; so much for putting him over my shoulder and getting him to burp. I dare say he burps if he drinks too much beer. But his girlfriend is in a better position to know that than I. Especially since they moved in together last year.

Finn and Natalie live with their two dogs in Bendigo. They both work hard and have a full social life. I'm relieved he doesn't have a phobia of the average lifestyle. When I was his age, I did everything to be different, when all I was doing was conforming to the mob anyway.

He's brought the dogs with him to my place. We walk them to the top of the hill in the forest reserve.

"Got something to tell you, Mum."

"Yeah?"

"I'm going to propose to Natalie."

Perhaps it was because he knew I would whoop with joy that he waited until we were in the bush, as far away from people as possible. I fling my arms around him. "My darling boy, I've been hoping and praying this would happen!"

We can see the whole of Castlemaine from where we're standing. It's like having reached the top of a mountain. He and I were a sole-parent family with no money, property or status in society. But he knows how to love someone, enough to want to marry them. I taught him what really matters. And he is, I know, worthy of being loved. I have the feeling that she will say yes.

Like I said, so much for putting him over my shoulder and getting him to burp; it's hard to believe that was twenty-six years ago …

*T*hings were speeding up now. The doctor was lying next to me on the seagrass matting in our lounge room. It surprised me that a man could be so helpful at a time like that. Perhaps he just wanted me to stop making so much noise. He looked into my face, telling me when to breathe deeply, relax, push, breathe …

My then husband John was in the kitchen making soup, keeping an ear on how things were going. Meanwhile, my tuned-in New-Age friends pampered me with massage, encouragement, incense and made awe-struck comments about a new day dawning. I'd never stayed awake long enough to see a sunrise; finally I had, and I couldn't have cared less.

"Won't be long now," the doctor said pointedly as John entered the room. Our son was on the way.

Our 'child' would have been more correct at that point. We had both made it quite clear we didn't want to know the sex of the baby. I had also made it clear I didn't want drugs or gas. Had that been the right decision?

Yes, of course! I remonstrated with myself silently for the moment of weakness. There was nothing more I could do about it anyway, the baby was coming. It was lucky we lived far enough away from the neighbours. I had tested that belief well prior to the birth: "On Thursday at 7pm I'm going to yell as loud as I can. If you hear me, call us." Nobody had called. Very soon I was going to put it to the test again.

Tom was a qualified home-birth doctor. Even so, how could he truly understand the reason I'd started screaming instead of yelling? But there he was, still lying next to me, willing me to summon every ounce of energy. Composure restored, I got into a squatting position.

Go on, make it hurt some more. See if I care.

That would have been my thought if I'd allowed myself energy to think.

"It's a boy!"

"WAAAAAAAAaaaaaaaaahhhhhh!"

Exclamations of joy, tears of happiness, sighs of relief, kisses on cheeks and faces, everyone hugging everyone else. Apart from the pain, it had been a marvellous experience. 'Cosmic.' 'Positive.' 'Empowering.'

He was washed and wrapped in a towel, a picture was taken. Finley Johnathon McAllister, the reason for all the fuss, had arrived.

Before we go on, I need to explain my background and the effect it had on me and my life. The ripple effect of war is real. It doesn't stop with the person who fought or was bombed. The trauma never goes away and is passed on to future generations, possibly further than just the next in line, although Finn doesn't seem to have suffered too badly. Perhaps that's because I sought therapy, whereas the generation before mine was taught to soldier on, get on with it and get over it.

My mother's side of the family were from Russia originally, her father having moved away after the revolution. My grandmother on Mum's side never referred to their family as Russian. But it has come to light that the reason for that is rooted in World War Two days. Living in Latvia, you would never refer to yourself as Russian. If you did, you would be sent back to Russia, and you didn't want that. They were 'white Russians' or Tsarists rather than 'red Russians' or Communists.

Imagine a twelve-year-old girl in Latvia, Northern Europe, in the 1930s; living with her parents, sister and grandmother; ice-skating in the winter, moving to their holiday house in summer, going to church every Sunday. Walking for hours picking berries in forests where pine trees are native to the land. Learning to sing and play the piano. Finding out another world war has just started.

At four o'clock one morning there's a commotion at their front door. The family cowers behind her father as two Russian soldiers draw their rifles.

"You. Come with us."

They never see him again.

During the war, Russians captured civilians and sent them to Gulag labor camps to be worked like dogs until they dropped dead. Such was the fate of my grandfather Andrei Vasilev. After the war, Mum and her family spent years in a German refugee camp. From there they were asked by the Australian government if they wanted to start a new life here. Of course they did, but nothing could undo what had been done to them.

On the surface, and to those who have no idea what she went through, you would think she has never looked back. She embraced Australian citizenship, put the past behind her and made a new life for herself. This was made possible by strength, tenacity and stubbornness that has taken me fifty years to appreciate rather than criticise. In another very real sense however, she has looked back every day.

The culture shock she experienced didn't happen straight away. Conservatism dominated the Australia she and her family came to in the fifties. Robert Menzies, prime minister of the day, made no secret of his anti-communist sentiments. Mum and her family would have felt right at home. They didn't have to worry anymore. Mum and Dad met, married and began their suburban life. Dad was an unendingly patient, loving man. Personally I think he should be made a saint and put in the Australian Lectionary: *St Douglas of suburban Melbourne; husband, father, worker, Labor voter, Richmond supporter, good bloke, d. 2012.*

In the sixties, society started changing. Many things that, up until that point, had been taboo subjects suddenly became suitable for conversation; sex and drugs and rock 'n' roll. Music changed. In the words of Plato: "*When the music changes, the walls of the city shake.*" Conscientious objectors protested against Vietnam. There were alterations to the White Australia policy. Men grew their hair. Women wanted equal pay. People like my mother and her family didn't see why women should be working at all. That's about where I come into the picture.

In the seventies, the Whitlam Labor government introduced changes to Australian society that altered it irrevocably and for the better; for all 'men and women of Australia'. While Dad was quietly pleased about this, Mum's side of the family was horrified ... staunch right-wingers, they disapproved vehemently of the 'commos'. Reds under the bed were still seen by many as a real threat and not welcome in any home of hers. This often led to heated debates between my parents, usually ending with Dad bowing out gracefully, rolling a smoke, sticking it behind his ear, putting a box of matches in his pocket and going down to his veggie garden to see what needed doing.

After what she'd been through, Mum had to have control of everything around her. This became more obvious as our society kept changing, and even more obvious as I started to emerge from my cocoon. Growing up in the late sixties and early seventies I had been taking in what I observed around me.

All of it.

Not just the straight-laced suburban bits. The other stuff as well. Skinheads, sharpies, shouting neighbours, blokes, sheilas, short skirts, bell-bottom pants, tight jeans, *Number 96*. And music; music that was meant to be played loud. AC/DC, Rose Tattoo, Black Sabbath, Pink Floyd, Midnight Oil, The Angels.

Part of Mum had remained in Latvia and had no intention of leaving. Her culture dictated that if you were a girl you were modest, quiet and churchgoing. Your destiny was to meet a man, settle down and have children with him: The End.

She was so intent on molding me into a modest, quiet girl that she tolerated nothing less. By sixteen I knew I had no choice but to leave home as soon as I could. It was more than teenage rebellion, although that certainly played a part.

There had never been any question of what I would do with my life. It didn't occur to anyone that I might not want to do what everyone else did. That meant two things; firstly, that many in my family were devastated when I left home or, to be more specific, without having found a husband first. Secondly, it meant I had virtually no skills for adjusting to the new environment I found myself in. Even though I was perceptive enough to know I had to leave the situation I was in, I was now fair game, innocent, clueless.

After moving out, I found energy I never knew I had. As a tram conducting, peace campaigning hippy, I went to poetry readings and regularly marched down the main street of Melbourne in political demonstrations. And let's not be precious about it; being a party animal took energy too. It was something I learned very well and there were plenty of people more than willing to coach me. But the less said about that the better.

Rose Tattoo, the Angels, Yothu Yindi, Midnight Oil and Black Douglas scotch defined the basis of my social life. The Tatts' gigs were the most affordable, so my friends and I saw them often. It was a far cry from modest, quiet or churchgoing.

It is in this brain-cell-destroying context that the distance between the family and I became set in stone, especially as I became closer to John; even though it was he who took me away from the party-hard scene. He was a peace campaigning hippy as well, worked in a community house and spent his free time reading and meditating. Love at first sight is real. But love or not, he was a hippy. Our desire to marry was seen by some on Mum's side of the family as outrageous in the extreme. Nobody listened to what Dad said about it; their minds were made up.

"Anna, you cannot be serious!"

"I am actually, Mum." We had set a date to be united; that is, to officially declare to the world that we were bed-buddies as well as friends, but not in a traditional church setting. We had chosen the forest area around Healesville for the ceremony and had enlisted the help of one of John's friends who was a spiritual minister of no particular denomination. He was a kind-hearted fellow as I recall, but in the eyes of my mother and her family, he was the devil incarnate, as was John.

"It iss disgusting," she said in her heaviest European accent. Just to make sure she had made the point she said it again.

"*Disgusting.*"

Later down the track, our son Finn would soften the blow, as kids inadvertently do in these situations. But in the meantime, the rules were the rules. The man you were expected to settle down with as a modest Latvian girl – you had to *marry* him; in the church. I didn't pretend not to understand. It was also preferable for the man you married to be Russian Orthodox. That meant not Catholic, Anglican, etcetera. If he were any religion other than Christian or, God forbid, an atheist, he wouldn't be considered human. How my father had made it onto the radar I don't know. He was Church of England and a leftie as well. Perhaps they had adapted to Australian society more than I'd given them credit for.

*B*ring up a child in this?

I was walking down Chapel Street Prahran contemplating single motherhood. Six months after Finn was born, John chickened out and ran off to Mullumbimbi with another, more suitable soulmate. The signs had been there long before Finn was born; I'd just been too scared to look. The family had given me a mixture of sympathy and 'I-told-you-so, what-did-you-expect'.

Stella was tall, tranquil and had dark hair that she wore in a long plait. She was a fellow peace campaigner and, until I had become a mother, a fellow party-goer too. I stopped in the middle of the street holding the handle of the pram and said, "I can't do this."

"Bit late for that, isn't it?" she observed uneasily.

"I mean bringing him up here, in the city." I had to move away. It had come like a bolt of lightning. I knew I'd never had a clearer thought. We both headed for a seat.

There were ads on every shop window, bus, tram, and lamp post. Car exhausts mingled with pub smells and garbage bins. Everyone was intent on getting somewhere, oblivious to the noise, exhaust fumes and each other. People honked their horns for the slightest breach of traffic etiquette.

"What brought this on?" she asked.

"Look at it." I gestured to the bedlam in front of us.

"You've just had a baby."

"Go to the top of the class."

"What I'm trying to say is your hormones have changed."

"Exactly, and I have to listen to what they're telling me."

I would miss her.

Perhaps Dad's mother had been looking down from heaven, urging me on. Just as I had never met Mum's dad, I had never met Dad's mum either. She had died of TB when he was young. They would quite happily have stayed in Shepparton but moved to Melbourne to find work. Being in the city was a stark contrast to what they were used to. Dad had grown up in a house that backed on to a creek. He and his brothers had known the bush around them like the back of their hands. I had never known the bush that way. But the epiphany, or whatever it had been, made me suspect it wouldn't be that hard to learn.

"Uncle Jim!" I exclaimed.

"What about him?"

"He lives in the country."

Dad's brother James couldn't stomach the city and had moved back to the country as soon as he could. Dad probably would have done the same if he had not met Mum. But Mum wasn't going to live in the country, even if you paid her. Dad lost touch with his brother because of the distance between them and Mum's unwillingness to go 'gallivanting around'. Uncle Jim still visited a couple of times a year. If his handwriting was as atrocious as Dad's, letter writing was not an option. Thankfully, phones in the seventies had closed the gap. Finn and I could become a link between Dad and him, and I was sure he would help me with childminding occasionally.

He lived just outside of Bendigo. It was there, or close to there, that we would have to move. It was the perfect solution.

After a few phone calls, Carol, a friend from Melbourne who had a house in Maldon, asked us if we wanted to rent the two spare rooms she had.

That's how I found myself driving down the main street in Maldon, Central Victoria at three in the morning with Finn asleep in his car seat and our furniture on a trailer behind. Arriving there was like being transported into the 1800s, rabbits and all, twenty of them in my field of vision at any one time.

"Oh no!" I gasped as I slammed on the brakes. Myxamatosis, the virus introduced to curb rabbit numbers, didn't work anymore. The calicivirus had not yet been introduced. It didn't take long to grasp the fact that nobody in Maldon cared about the bunnies. The usual response to an oh-my-god-I-almost-hit-a-rabbit story was, "Put your high beam lights on next time," spoken with a menacing undertone.

Carol was a quiet, self-contained woman who had worked in halfway houses, did yoga and meditated. She was between jobs when we moved in and so was introduced to the one-sided world of the infant by day and by night. Finn was yelling the place down in the next room, where I had put him as a result of a tantrum he was having.

"He's got a good pair of lungs on him," she observed.

"Ready to stop that yet, Finn? Stop making so much noise and I'll let you out."

"NnnnnnnnnnnnnnO!"

"Okay. I'm here, so let me know when you wanna come out."

"NnnnnnnnnnnnnO!"

"And determined with it," said Carol.

"Yep. He has spirit. He'll use it to his advantage one day."

It wasn't the first time he'd been put in the spare room and it wouldn't be the last.

"You'll be able to negotiate with him one of these days."

"Yeah? Looking forward to that. Finn! Come on, settle down. Don't you want to come back out here now?"

"NnnnnnnnnnnnnnO!"

Laugh at It

We could have lived at Carol's as long as we wanted. She was more than happy for us to be there. Maldon was charming and quiet – too quiet. Finn and I moved twenty kilometres down the road to Castlemaine. But the nice places were too expensive for us, got sold, or the owners would decide to move in themselves. Then there were the other ones …

There was one place I flatly refused to stay in. You don't negotiate with a neighbour who comes over, dressed in only a towel, inviting you over for a drink. You move. Thankfully, the estate agents understood. Then there was the grey brick unit. I suspected some prisons were brighter to live in. We moved when the lease expired.

The house after that was the final straw. We shared it with another single mother. Her four-year-old boy had Attention Deficit Disorder which she refused to do anything about, believing it to be 'just a stage' he was going through.

"How would it be if Finn and I moved back in for a few months?" I asked Carol over the phone. "I hate asking, but we need to look around and find something good this time. If we take the first place we find and it's anything like the last two, I think I'll go mad."

"Not a problem," said Carol. "When do you want to move?"

"Five minutes?"

She put forward an alternative suggestion, "What about the weekend?"

"I think I can stand it for another four days." Just then a car pulled up outside.

"Oh shit." One of the boy's friends had come for an afternoon of fun and mayhem. It was time to fasten down anything that could be picked up and thrown.

"They're home. The vibe's not the best around here since I told her I was thinking we should move. I've got to go and get Finn too." He was in grade prep. "I'll call you tomorrow, okay?"

We were stacking furniture and boxes in the garage. "I had heard of Attention Deficit Disorder, but I had no idea what it was really like," I told her.

"I shared a house with a single mum who had two kids that both had it. They bounced off each other when they weren't bouncing off the walls."

"Maybe ADD didn't even exist before processed food. Alice feeds her son chocolate, lollies and fizzy drinks whenever he asks for them. Then she wonders why he starts going berserk half an hour later. I would say to her 'Look, can't you see the connection?' She'd say, 'Oh, all those don't-eat-this, don't-eat-that people are a bunch of crackpots.'"

"In other words, she was saying you were a crackpot? That must have been awkward! Finn, are you glad you moved away from there?" Carol wanted to know.

"Yes," he said emphatically. "He was breaking all my toys and taking them and not giving them back. And his Mum didn't tell him off. And he made so much noise," he recalled, smiling and shaking his head.

"Well, I'll only play with your toys if you let me, and I certainly won't break them," she said reassuringly. Finn looked relieved.

We now officially didn't have anywhere of our own to live. At least we didn't have to couch-surf. Even so, not having a stable home put us both under stress. This was starting to show for me as strange vague-outs that would happen sporadically and for no particular reason.

Emma was a slight, pretty, effervescent woman. We'd met at the local community house. She was one of those people who knew how to strike up conversation, which is what she had done that day. We had made friends instantly. Finn and her boy James played together regularly.

It was sole-parents pension day and we were in the supermarket. As we strolled down one of the aisles, something came over me that seemed to pre-empt the vague-outs, something I had started calling The Feeling. It was like I'd been in that supermarket before, which of course I had. But this was more than physical recognition. It was a sense of having been in that place, at that exact *time,* same people, same things happening. Maybe I had dreamt it?

"You alright?" Emma wanted to know.

"Why?"

"You went funny just then. You stopped walking and started staring into space. You okay?"

I didn't know what to say.

"Come on. Let's find somewhere to sit down." She tried to make me sit on the bench they provided next to the deli section.

"I have to do the shopping. I can't leave the trolley here."

"Take your bag, then."

"No, no it's okay."

She didn't seem convinced. "Are you sure you're alright?"

"Yeah, I'm fine. You know that thing that happens sometimes? That feeling of deja vu ? You get that, don't you?"

"Yes, we all get that from time to time. But nobody's ever told me I was staring into space when it's happened to me. You kind of went somewhere else."

It had been happening a lot lately. But I didn't tell her that. I also didn't tell her I had arranged to go and talk to someone at the Buddhist centre in Bendigo about it.

Lyn, elegant with short white hair, was someone else I'd met since moving from Melbourne. A Buddhist, she went to their centre to attend meditation sessions and workshops on the Buddhist way of life. When Uncle Jim had Finn on weekends, I sometimes went there with her. A calm, serene person, she had a love for all things spiritual. She had suggested I talk to one of the monks about the vague-outs I'd been having.

"I'll go to the temple, do a bit of meditation, go to the kitchen and make myself a cup of tea. You take as long as you need, okay?"

The monks' quarters were as basic as I expected they would be. The common lounge room had very few pictures to adorn the walls. Any that were there were photographs of lakes or rainforests with quotes from the Dalai Lama elegantly printed on them. The monk I had come to see was lanky, middle-aged and, of course, calm and gentle in temperament.

"I was trying to think of the right words to describe what it feels like when I have one of these things. This is what I came up with," I told him. On the paper I gave him were descriptions such as *'Celestial, impalpable, airy, not of this world, light-headed (but not dizzy), intangible ...'*

"Laugh at it," he advised after reading it.

I must have looked taken aback. He looked like he meant it.

"Um... I'm too scared to laugh at it? What if they get worse?"

"You don't know that they will. That's just creating extra anxiety on top of what you're already experiencing." He said it with the same air of calmness and assurance he used for everything else. Maybe it really was that simple.

"Detachment. That's what you're on about, isn't it?" I said.

He smiled. "I've found detachment a worthwhile skill to have.

It helps me put things into perspective and in that way deal with whatever issues arise."

"Hmm." It was something they talked about all the time at the Buddhist centre. I didn't think I was getting any closer to achieving it myself. How many times had I sat in the gompa with those calm Buddhists, trying to be as self-contained as they were? I was always more interested in the way that woman wore her hair in a bun (always so perfect) or the line of that man's head (some guys can get away with shaving their head but some just so can't), or how straight that person was sitting (and for such a long time).

"Detachment comes with practice," he told me. "You can't will it to happen. You have to work at it. Meditation is one way of attaining it. But there are other ways."

Meditation had obviously suited him down to the ground. Everything about him suggested serenity. Road rage? Complaining to a supermarket cashier? Impatience with a child? Never. Of course he wouldn't be allowed to have children of his own in his situation. It was ludicrous. People like him were the very ones the world needed more of.

"These turns you've told me about, how do they manifest? What happens when you have one?" he asked.

"I vague out. It's not like I pass out or collapse or anything. But I'm not really present. While I'm in that state, I might as well be asleep."

"How long do they last?"

"I don't know really. It's hard to tell. A few seconds? That's what people tell me."

"You say you might as well be asleep. Does everything feel like a dream? Or is it more like being unconscious?"

"It's like being unconscious. I vague out then come back to reality. I don't remember anything. People tell me I start talking to myself. Maybe I've had them when I'm alone and don't even know it."

"Sounds like temporal lobe epilepsy."

I looked at him with alarm.

"But that's just what it sounds like. I'm not saying I know what it is. Not by any means. If you want to find out once and for all what these things are, you should visit your doctor and ask to have tests done to find out."

"They won't do that. Not unless they think there's a good reason. They couldn't care less." I knew I was frowning, being negative. I knew that contrasted with what he was on about. Then again I had no plans to become a nun. We talked for a while longer. Before I left, he once again suggested I see a doctor. I thanked him for listening.

"That's quite alright," he said. "Remember – laugh at it."

"I'll try," I promised him, doubtful as to whether or not I would be able to.

"He really meant it. 'Laugh at it,' he said. He said it twice," I told Lyn as we drove back to Castlemaine.

"They're pretty cluey people those Buddhists," she said.

"Yeah, I'll say. No talking for the sake of it. Think before they say anything, don't they?"

"Yes, that's true. He was a doctor before he decided to become a monk."

"Oh!"

"What's wrong?"

"When he suggested going to have tests, I told him I didn't think the doctors could care less!"

Lyn was almost as calm as a Buddhist nun herself. "Oh, I don't think he'd take offence. I'm sure he knows what you meant."

"Hope so," I said distractedly. He was a doctor. He knew what he was talking about when he said 'temporal lobe epilepsy'. Laugh at it?

Ha-ha.

58 Green Street

It had been almost seven years since I'd moved away from Melbourne. Stella had become a single mother during that time, and she was visiting me in Castlemaine on a weekend 'off' from being a parent. Finn was at Uncle Jim's, so we were out having dinner.

"This is something I used to take for granted. Just going out and having something to eat with my friends; especially when I had a job and I could afford it."

"Yeah, that's for sure," I agreed. "And now it's hard not to feel guilty for spending money on myself when there's so little of it. And for wanting time away from my kid! I hate feeling like that. I love Finn to bits."

"I know you do. I get the same about Cynthia. It's not that I don't love her to bits. She's the best thing that ever happened to me. It's not about needing to be away from them. It's about just having some time out; nothing wrong with that."

I nodded in understanding. We sat for a while thinking about the kids we were feeling so guilty about and sipping jasmine tea.

"Tonight is full moon," I said, looking at the evening sky from the window of the Vietnamese restaurant. "They say it's a bad time for epileptics. Not that I'm epileptic or anything …" I couldn't get what the Buddhist monk had said out of my head.

"No, you're not." She looked at me, puzzled, wondering where that had come from.

"I went to see this Buddhist monk to talk about those funny turns I've been having. Lyn told me about a particular fellow; said I should talk to him. It turns out he was a doctor before he became a monk, but she didn't tell me that until I'd spoken to him."

"What did he say?"

"I gave him a list of things I feel when I have the turns, and he asked a few questions. He said it sounds like epilepsy. Not that it *was* epilepsy, just what it sounded like. But whatever it is that's causing these things, I had another one yesterday."

"Have you been to the doctor?"

"Yes. They've sent me to get tests for blood sugar, hypoglycemia, diabetes and liver function."

"Parenting can be very stressful."

"Especially on your own," I said. "But I haven't got to tell you that. Especially now you're doing it on your own too."

"Oh God," she said rolling her eyes. "You want to hear the latest? Cynthia's friend Jackie got a dog last weekend. Now all she can think about is getting one too." Stella's daughter Cynthia was four. "She keeps asking, and I tell her we can't have one because the landlord won't let us have dogs. But she doesn't understand why he's telling us we can't have a dog. Then I explain that it's his house, and she asks me why he's not living there. I tell her it's because we're living there, and she asks why he isn't living there with us, so then I try to explain …"

I smiled as she described the situation, took another sip of jasmine tea and relaxed. I still hadn't found somewhere for Finn and me to live, but we hadn't outstayed our welcome at Carol's.

The cleaning job I had on Wednesdays in Castlemaine meant I had a spare hour before getting Finn from school. Emma was home, as I suspected she would be. There were visitors as well, as was usually the case.

I had come to the conclusion that people could be divided into two groups: the visit*ors* and the visit*ed*. Part of this theory was that family ties, or the lack of them, were largely responsible for the difference. My theory was fraught with generalizations the size of meteor craters. Even so, I had a feeling I was onto something.

If you're from a close-knit family, the perfectly reasonable need to have your existence validated will quite likely come from there. But if family dynamics are strained, a person may need to find that validation elsewhere – friends, community groups, work, religious groups, sport, etc.

My family wasn't exactly ringing the phone off the wall. I had been making my own 'family' ever since leaving home and had come to another conclusion; blood is *not* thicker than water. Emma was one of my 'relatives'.

Content to be at home and potter around, she was a perfect example of the 'visited' person in my theory. Although far from a hermit, she did not seem to have the same need as someone like me to actively search out the company of others. From a family that included six sisters, countless nieces and nephews, not to mention friends, there was always someone there. You knew you could drop in, and you knew what kind of reception you would get. The kettle seemed to be perpetually on at 58 Green Street.

Maggie, Kelly, Sue, myself and others spent many hours over the years at Emma's kitchen table drinking coffee, some smoking cigarettes, others eating biscuits. Many hours were spent talking about kids, society, politics, sex, the lack of it, men/women, the lack of them, music, money, or how to fix the latest broken car/washing machine/leaking tap. It was a congregation point for single mothers. Kids would play close by, usually happily. However our conversations were often broken into fragments …

"They had to have their dog put down," Emma was telling us.

"Oh no!" I exclaimed.

"Not Sprout, he was so cute," said someone else.

"Yeah, I know, but he was really sick ... Hey, don't scribble over his drawing, that's not nice. Come on, stop that ... what was I saying?"

"They had to have Sprout put down," someone reminded her sadly.

"Yeah, so they had to pay the vet up front," said Emma.

"But I thought they let you pay those kinds of things off," said someone else, "or even do it for free ... Hey, stop that will ya?"

A scuffle over some drawing paper was brewing over by the couch. Someone would have to intervene.

"Come over here, darling," said Kelly, mother of one of the kids who had been bickering. "Look at this book we got from the library. It's got some great pictures in it." Little ones, unlike teenagers, fall for the distraction ploy. Both children were soon entranced as Kelly read the story, pointing to the corresponding pictures.

Peace was restored, the kettle filled and put on the stove.

A week later, I visited Emma again to fill in the spare hour. She looked like she had something to tell me.

"We're moving," she said, with a you're-not-going-to-believe-this grin on her face.

"No way!" It wasn't something she would have decided on lightly. "When? Why? Where?"

"In two months. I found a cheap house in Castlemaine to buy and decided it was too good to walk away from. The bank will lend me most of the money, and Mum and Dad will lend me the rest."

"Fantastic. Well, I know you've got lots of people to help you, but if you need another one ...?" She'd need all the help she could get. She had accumulated 'stuff'. There was something else I wanted to say. She said it for me.

"I know you've been worried about finding a good place to live. Do you want to take over the lease for this place?"

"*Yes*," I said without hesitation. It was the perfect solution.

"*Found* somewhere to live," I said flippantly, as I walked into Carol's kitchen.

Carol laughed with surprise. "Already? How did you manage that?"

"58 Green Street. Emma's buying a house."

"She's *moving?*"

"Yeah, can you believe it?"

"And she needs someone to take over the lease?"

"Yep."

"When can you move in?"

"Well ... that's the thing. She won't be moving for two months. But it's perfect. It's just what we need. Can we stay here until then?"

"Of course you can."

"Thank you." I went over to her and hugged her.

"No problem," she said as she reciprocated the hug.

I sighed with relief. "I've got a good feeling about this place."

Finally, the waiting was over for Emma. She was moving into her own home. We'd been packing things all morning. It was time for a break.

"Coffee?" she asked.

I nodded.

"I'll hire a carpet shampoo machine tomorrow when everything's been moved," she said, looking at the floor that hadn't seen daylight for ten years. "Let's have this coffee outside."

On the front porch, I told her, "It'll be good to move in here. It might mean I'm not as stressed out as I've been lately. I've been having those funny turns for a while now."

"Well, don't do any more today. You've helped me so much already."

"I don't get them because of doing too much. I don't know what the reason is. They're like deja vu. But they only come on occasionally, out of the blue for no reason. You remember that time in the supermarket? "

"Yes I do. I was worried about you that day. Have you been to the doctor?"

"Yeah."

"What did he say?"

"I've had tests for liver function, diabetes, all that sort of thing. It's all fine."

"That's good."

"Yeah, it's good. I'm finding out what the turns aren't. But I still don't know what they are."

"How often do they happen?"

"It varies. I still don't know why." I told Emma about one of the most recent episodes. "It must look weird when I have one. It feels weird. Kind of like I'm there but I'm not; conscious but not completely."

"That's what it looked like the time I saw you have one. You had any more since the one you just told me about?"

"Yes."

"When was the last one you had?"

"Last week," I told her.

"Stress?"

"Probably. Mum and I had an argument the day before I had the most recent one. She doesn't want Finn and me to visit at Christmas anymore."

Emma gasped. "You're joking."

"True Christian, huh? Says family is the most important thing, then tells her only daughter and grandson not to come and celebrate the birth of Jesus."

"Did she give a reason?"

"Says it's all too much." I had long ago stopped trying to understand what drove her. It was too complicated. She probably didn't know what it was herself.

"All too much, that's a bit obscure, isn't it? What does she mean by that?" she asked.

"Whatever she wants it to mean. Whatever she needs it to mean. Her need to have control of everything around her has never gone away."

"Because of the war?" Emma knew the story.

"Yeah, she says she can still see her father's face as he looked at her one last time before they took him away; like he was taking a picture of her. I probably told you they sent him to Siberia."

Emma nodded.

"His name is inscribed on a monument on the site where the gulag was."

"God," Emma said in disgust. "We can't begin to know what that's like."

"True. But enough of that pleasant cheerful stuff …"

"No, what do you mean? It's part of who you are. It's part of who she is."

I sat in silence for a few moments. "There would be something wrong with a person who didn't have emotional scars as a result of something like that happening to them. But she refuses to acknowledge there could be anything wrong with *her*. Says there's nothing the matter with her, it's the Russians. And in a way, she's right."

"Yeah, but she's in Australia now. And what are you supposed to do for Christmas? I'd say come to our house, but we're going to Jill's place in Wangaratta." Jill was one of her many sisters.

"We'll figure out something. We're going to my Uncle's on Christmas Eve anyway. He's got some friends in Bendigo he's going to spend Christmas Day with. We can probably stay overnight and tag along next day."

"Thank goodness for that."

"I'll say. Mum did say it was just Christmas she doesn't want us to be at. We can go and see them in the New Year."

"Oh well, that makes it alright then," Emma said with sarcasm in her voice.

"Yeah, totally," I said just as sarcastically.

"She needs help," said Emma.

"Yep, everyone says that except her. Her family has been through a war. All other life problems pale into insignificance in comparison.

So no more Christmas at Mum and Dad's and we just have to suck it up and deal with it."

"That's not right."

"No, it's not, is it?"

Christmas that year turned out better than we thought. Uncle Jim, Finn and I went to the Salvation Army and helped cook a roast dinner for people who had nobody at all to spend Christmas with. In the New Year, Finn and I visited Mum and Dad at a time that was, for whatever reason, more acceptable to Mum. While we were there we exchanged belated Christmas presents, most of which went into an op-shop box when I started packing again.

"Thank God it's all done."

Emma had just helped me move the last load of furniture into the place that had been hers. We sat among the bean bags and boxes.

"You've still got to unpack it all," she reminded me.

"That's the fun part."

"Really?" she said dubiously. Emma didn't share my love of this stage of the moving experience.

"Of course, decor is very important. I have to get it all unpacked and put away anyhow, before I can get back into my relaxation routine. I'm meant to be finding my inner sanctum or some bloody thing."

"Did the doctor tell you to make time to relax?"

"Yeah, said there was nothing they could pinpoint that was causing the turns. So I told him I would take time out each day to meditate and relax."

"How's that going?"

"Ha! It's not. That's just what I *told* him I would do. I wasn't bullshitting when I said it to him. I have tried. Meditation's just not my thing. Maybe you're not supposed to try. Maybe that's where I'm going wrong."

"Possibly, you need as few distractions as possible. And you need to do it at the same time every day. Or so I'm told."

"That's what I was told, too. I'll start, and it might go alright for a few minutes, but next thing, I've completely forgotten what I'm doing, and I'm thinking about what I'm going to cook for dinner or what Finn's got on after school."

"Well, at least it doesn't seem to be anything serious."

"The doctor said if what I have is mild epilepsy, it would be from that accident in the eighties." In my 'party animal' days I'd been a passenger in a car that skidded off the road. "And that something has to happen for it to get worse, something specific like meningitis, encephalitis or another head injury. It doesn't spread like a germ."

"Right."

"He also said the head injury I got from that accident is mild in comparison to what happens to some people."

"You mean like Marie?"

"Yeah, like Marie." Marie was a woman she knew who had crashed her car and been made a paraplegic.

"I'm glad you don't have to go through what she goes through every day." She came over and gave me a hug.

"Thank you. Wanna cuppa tea?"

"Yes, please."

The tea and cups were the first things I'd unpacked.

"The doctor also said epilepsy and stress are related. That stress can bring on epilepsy and he commended me for taking up meditation, even though I haven't really, and said he was glad I wasn't going to be taking any of those medicines they prescribe for epilepsy. They make your hair fall out. You get sick in the guts …"

"Yuck."

"Yes. But never mind, I'm not going to have to take it. I'm not epileptic.

School holidays had started. Finn and I had settled into 58 Green Street. We were going out to do some shopping, or at least I was.

"Come on, time to go."

"No, Mum. Can't I stay home?"

"No, you're too young to stay at home by yourself."

That annoyed him. He was a boy, therefore he was invincible.

"Come on, Finn!" Six was not old enough by a long shot.

"Owwwwww, Muuum!" Some gestures and movements are the same in all children, like the stamp of the foot combined with a sudden slackness of the body. On this occasion it seemed to be more for show than actual protest.

I'd named our yellow car The Lemon. It was. We got in and I turned the key. It was in a good mood and decided to start. We arrived at our first stop, a second-hand warehouse.

"G'day."

"G'day."

The guy who ran it was a man of few words, someone you saw down the street all the time without knowing his name. But he always said g'day, even if you never got more than that out of him.

"The furniture section's over there, isn't it?"

"Yep."

We needed some nice furniture, especially a comfortable couch. I sat in a purple four-seater that caught my eye.

"How much is this one?"

"Eighty bucks."

That would be pushing it. But it was worth every cent. I inspected it more closely.

"I'll take it. Do you deliver?"

"Yep. Tomorrow okay?"

"Tomorrow's fine."

Rich purple. Not seventies yellow with lime-green and orange dots. Not middle-class beige. Or white with coffee stains. Or bogan-black with rips and cigarette burns. A plush four-seater purple couch. Like the bed in Goldilocks, it was 'just right'. A cushion put in the right place and you wouldn't even realise one of the buttons was missing.

"You like it?"

"Yeah, Mum, looks good. Can you buy this for me, please?" He'd found a toy truck.

"I'll chuck that in for nothing," said the owner. It was the longest sentence I'd ever heard him say.

On the same day, we found something even better than a couch. Around the corner from us was a family who had ads up around town about their three litters of kittens. They were giving them away. A woman wearing a flannelette shirt and trackie daks answered the door.

"Yeah?" she said through the cigarette in her mouth.

"Hi. I'm Anna. This is my son Finn. I called about the kittens yesterday. Could we have a look at them?"

"Yeah, sure. They're mostly out the back in the laundry. But they're all over the house really. If you want one, take one, for Christ sake." She showed us down the corridor and went back into the lounge room to watch TV. We didn't have to look for the kittens. They really were everywhere, and you smelt them before you saw them. The place reeked of cigarettes, cats, cat shit, dogs, dog shit, greasy food, and marijuana. We would be doing one of these kittens a favour taking it away.

"I suppose this is better than drowning them ..."

"What, Mum?"

"Nothing, luv, nothing! Look, what about that one?" I said, pointing to a sleek black kitten. It hissed at another one as they passed each other. "Or perhaps not that one ..."

After a while, I sat down on the floor of the sunroom, overwhelmed by the smell. The high-pitched meows came mainly from the laundry where the food and kitty litter trays were. With Finn standing nearby covering his nose, a fluffy grey apparition approached us. Her eyes were fixed on us, as if to say *I'm the one you want. Let not your hearts be troubled, for today you have been chosen – by me.* But it came out as, "Muuuuuwww."

It was love at first sight all around. We named her Sheba.

"She's so cute, Mum." Finn was cuddling our new grey friend adoringly. She meowed as if to say "Yes I am, aren't I?"

*S*chool holidays were finished. After dropping Finn off, I came home and sat on a chair on the front porch. I didn't eat, drink, write, think or read. I sat for an hour looking at the trees, the street and the sky. Sheba was purring on my lap, as relaxed as I was. The postman rode up and I went to take the letters from him.

"Thanks."

"No worries."

There was a bill and a handwritten letter. I recognised the writing but couldn't place it immediately. It was from my cousin Sonia.

It turned out the reason Mum didn't want Finn and I over for Christmas was because someone in the family had found a man, a straight-laced, respectable man whose views might have been too different from mine not to cause tension at the Christmas dinner table. This was never stated, but I knew my family. It was too much of a coincidence.

She had met him at a church function. They had become close straight away. But not too close, I was sure. Sonia, in stark contrast to me, believed in the family's version of what girls should do with their lives. So it went without saying that no hanky-panky would occur until the nuptials had taken place. Even I believed they would stick to this rule. The date had been set and Finn and I had been invited.

*I*t was a conservative affair. I'd never seen more blue rinses in one place at any one time. The hypocrisy never ceased to amaze me. Criticism flowed effortlessly from the mouths of people like this at the sight of punks and Goths who put blue in their hair, yet they did it themselves. Collectively, the handbags, clothes, jewellery and shoes these women were wearing would have been the financial equivalent of rent on our house until Finn turned eighteen. The most awkward thing about this gathering were the stares coming from the blue rinse set and their husbands. Not a word was said, there was no need. Finn and I were inferior in their eyes. We were wearing the best clothes we could get from the op-shop, but some of these people wouldn't have used them as cleaning rags. None of them knew I was down to coin after buying our train tickets, and they would not have had any sympathy if they did. At least we would get a free feed.

At that time, my cousin Sonia's brother Greg and I vied for the position of most irreverent in the family. We sat at the back of the church rather than the front with family members. Whether Greg realised this was the first of many faux pas we would commit that day, I don't know. I knew nothing of protocol at events like these, and it was probably just as well. When the hymns were sung, Greg tried to persuade me to stay seated when everyone else stood. I almost went along with him until I saw that, of course, every other person was standing, at which point I stood and so did he.

"I don't know why they don't let you smoke in these places," he whispered to me.

"Greg! For God's sake, it's their wedding," I said under my breath. He reluctantly agreed that this was the most important thing. Finn stood on the other side of me dressed in trousers, shirt and vest, behaving impeccably. I was very proud of him and made a mental note to tell him so later on. In the meantime, I took his hand and squeezed it.

I suspected Greg had not had an easy time with his father, Uncle Leo, although he didn't talk about it very much. Uncle Leo had been scarred by the war as well. He hated the Russians even more than Mum did. If Greg had been subject to the same incessant criticism I'd listened to all my life, I empathised.

His sister Sonia, on the other hand, could do no wrong. She had been a receptionist, went to church every Sunday, belonged to an embroidery guild and valued family over all else. For this she had been praised and, just as importantly, not criticised. If she had explored the comparatively free and easy Australian lifestyle she would have received the same condemnation as I had. But she had not and was now reaping the rewards of an obedient life.

Hymns were sung, rings exchanged, the blessing of the church given. The organ started playing again. They walked down the aisle aglow, the train of her dress extending behind her. This was the only time she would ever wear it. There was no question in anyone's minds about that. She and Brendan had 'tied the knot'. It was made of steel and welded. It would replace her chastity belt.

"Yes Anna, zat iss vot I mean. You should nott haff come if you had nussink decent to wear."

"That was my best dress," I retorted, which, I realised straight away, gave her more ammunition.

"Vell iff zat's your best dress, I vould hate to sink what your vorst dress iss."

"Mum, give it a rest!"

"Giff it a rest," she mimicked in her most sarcastic voice. Sometimes I felt like the adult in the relationship, but not at times like this. I wanted to stamp my foot and throw a tantrum, just like I'd done when I was two. We argued for a while longer and then said goodbye. Finn could not have failed to hear it. He came out from his room and sat with me, then got up and went to the bathroom, re-appearing a short time later with a wad of toilet paper in his hand. This was in case I needed to cry, which of course made me burst into tears.

"Thanks, darling."

"What was it about this time?"

"I wasn't wearing good enough clothes."

"At the wedding?"

"Yes. But she said you looked the best she's ever seen you."

"Uh-huh," he said, trying to hide his annoyance. Even at seven he was starting to tire of his grandmother's outbursts.

The Lemon usually started all right, but was developing a tendency to resist going into third gear.

"Come on, you bloody thing." I shouted, forgetting the window was down.

"Muuum!" Finn didn't want to be seen by his mates in a car with someone clearly insane.

"But things keep going wrong with this car!" I wasn't in the mood to refine my speech.

A few days later, I drove it to the garage in second, hoping people would understand. Someone behind me didn't and tooted their horn to let me know.

"Get stuffed, go around!"

Repairing the car was going to cost another two hundred dollars. Where was I going to get that? I'd only just paid them off for work on the radiator.

"We know you're good for it, Anna. Don't worry about it too much." They'd known us for years.

"Thanks, Pat. When do you think it'll be done?"

"Should be right to come and get it on Friday."

"Okay, see you then. And thanks again."

But even though I'd just been given credit by those nice people (again), it wasn't the relief I was telling myself it should be. There was always embarrassment associated with credit.

If I knew it was going to cost so much, I wouldn't have bought paint for the bedrooms. I certainly wouldn't have bought the carpet I had found for the lounge room. A business in town had done renovations and some of their old carpet was lying in the street. How naive I'd been. I went in and asked how much they wanted for it. They got sixty dollars from me. I could have gone with the trailer in the middle of the night and taken it for nothing.

In the meantime, Finn had learned to count to a hundred, the lounge room walls were white and the built-in cupboards were purple to match the couch. We put pictures on the walls, there were shelves for knick-knacks and the fireplace looked good, whether we were burning wood in it or not. I was keeping up with expenses and everything worked. Even if we didn't have a supportive family or a reliable car, we had a home.

*C*arol had just knocked at the door.

"Come in. It's just bangers and mash tonight, I couldn't afford to buy anything special for guests, sorry."

"That's alright," she said with a dismissive gesture.

"I did make sure we had enough tea though."

As we sat and drank I opened a book on tarot cards.

"Last night I was doing a clean-out and found some wedding photos. They brought back memories and I decided to do a tarot reading. Two cards dropped out of the pack before I had a chance to shuffle them even. Listen to this …"

"Hold on," she interrupted. "What was the question you were asking the cards?"

"Where am I headed in life? As in, what next?"

"Okay," she said.

"Six of Cups was one of them," I said, before reading from the book:

"*'Six of cups portrays Psyche seated on a rock…'*" In Greek mythology, Psyche is the Goddess of the Soul. "*'She holds a golden cup into which she pensively stares. In her right hand, she holds the rather bedraggled remains of her bridal bouquet.'*"

Carol's eyebrows went up.

"*'Her mysterious husband has flown away. The beautiful palace in which they lived has vanished and there is nothing left but pleasant memories. This is not an unhappy card.'*"

"Her mysterious husband has flown away …" She was amused by that.

"*'Through the past, Psyche has gained something precious.'*" I inclined my eyes and head over to Finn, who was on a bean bag, drawing.

"*'Despite loss, she knows something about herself and it is this truth that fosters the harmony we see in this card; stillness and serenity after a crisis in our lives.'*"

"That's very relevant. Sometimes it's scary just how relevant these things can be," Carol said.

"I'll say. It gets better. Queen of Wands." I read what the book said about the second card that had fallen out of the pack. "'*Queen Penelope has had to run the kingdom with only her young son to help her.*'"

"Wow," exclaimed Carol. Finn looked up for a moment then went back to drawing.

"'*She does not need a strong shoulder to lean on or socially acceptable label of wife to make her a worthwhile and confident individual.*'"

"It does make you wonder what's going on in the universe that we don't understand, doesn't it? How much more specific to the question could you get? Especially that last bit about her and her son running the kingdom," she said, gesturing with her arm to indicate the whole house. "Not needing to be married to have social status, very specific and very true."

I got up to make dinner. "A whole pack of cards," I said. "And without even having to shuffle them, that's the answer I got."

If I was somehow being 'told' something, perhaps it was that a cycle in life had been completed. The end of one cycle implies the beginning of another. I'd become more at peace with myself since becoming a mother. But if there's one thing I've learned in life, it's that nothing stays the same forever. Things change all the time. It was about to happen again.

Next Thing I Knew (1, 2)

I was headed for my cousin Greg's house. Finn was staying at a friend's place for the night. The plan was to stay at Greg's, go into the city next day, do some shopping and visit Stella. I was driving sedately on the Princes Highway in Caulfield.

Next thing I knew, I was in hospital.

"What's going on?"

"It's me, Anna" he said.

"Greg! How did you know I was here? Where am I?"

He started grinning like he thought I was mad. "You called half an hour ago."

"I did?"

"You don't remember?"

"I called you? No."

"You told me you were here, I said I'll be there in half an hour, and here I am."

How could I not have known that? Like a kid in the supermarket who's Mum has vanished, I suddenly felt very helpless.

*G*reg's house was minimalist; no excess furniture or clutter. With the wage he earned as an I.T. specialist he could have decked it out any way he wanted.

As he was pulling the bed out of his couch I said, "It's not like I remember doing it, but I'm glad I thought to call you instead of Mum and Dad."

A year after I had moved out of home, I accepted a lift from someone who should not have been driving. I'd received a head injury that night. Dad had been at the end of the hospital bed when I came to.

"It was bad enough for Dad last time something like this happened. He's too old for this kind of thing now."

"He's not that old yet."

"I suppose not. The point is, they can see me next time I come to Melbourne, when I'm standing there in front of them looking and feeling fine. The nurses reckon this time, if the car went ten centimeters further into the one in front I wouldn't be here to talk about it."

"Jesus. How did it happen?"

"One of my tyres blew out."

"And the other car?"

"They're fine, thank God. And yes, I do have third-party."

"Good."

"It's kind of a relief that it was a blowout."

"Why?"

"I thought it must have been one of those turns I was having; I thought they must be coming back. They stopped completely once Finn and I found somewhere permanent to live."

"What turns?"

"I told you about them."

"Tell me again."

I told him about the deja vu and going blank.

"Have you seen a doctor?"

"Oh yeah, he sent me to have tests. Said the results were inconclusive, told me to chill out. Lighten up. You know, like as if I've got nothing to stress about. I'm only a single mother after all," I said sarcastically.

"Lighten up? I'll give them 'lighten up' ..."

"So, what are you going to do about a car?"

"I need a loan. And there's only one place I can go for that – Mum and Dad." I cringed.

"You don't have a whole lot of options in your situation, do you? Oh well, good luck with that ..." he said, grinning.

"Ha ha, very funny," I said, seeing the grin. "The Lemon is a wreck. I'll get ninety dollars for it if I'm lucky ..."

"Ninety *dollars*?" he interjected. "I'd be surprised if you got ninety cents. That shit-box was a wreck before they sold it brand new."

Realizing how right he was, I groaned, put my hands to my face and shook my head. "I've just written off my car. I might get *twenty* dollars for it." I dared him with my eyes to suggest less than that. "I live in the country where there's practically no public transport. I've hit my head again. But I'm alive, not paralysed, and Finn wasn't in the car when it happened."

"I'm glad you're alright. Come on, let's go into the city and get something to eat."

"Good idea." I imagined calling Mum and Dad when I got home to tell them what happened. "Mum's gonna *freak* when I tell them about this."

"*O*h no, vott iss the matter?" Her European accent had not left her, even after fifty years in Australia.

"Hi, Mum. Why do you think something's the matter?" We hadn't said much more than 'hello'. Mothers know, as they say.

"Vell? Iss there?"

"There is, actually. But Finn and I are perfectly okay."

"Oh my Gott!" she exclaimed, my reassurance only fuelling the fire.

"Chill, Mum, okay? I was in an accident. The car's f... no good anymore, but we're fine. Finn wasn't even *in* the car."

"When? Where?"

"In Melbourne."

"Yoo vere in Melbourne? Vhy deedn't yoo say so?" Her accent seemed to deepen.

"It was just a quick trip, staying at Greg's and visiting a friend the next day, doing a bit of shopping, then going home. I'm sorry I didn't come and see you and Dad, I promise I will next time I'm in Melbourne."

"Yes, vell ..." Her voice took on the tone of a judge. "Zat's vot happenz, eezen't it?"

"Yep, sure thing Mum. Everyone who goes to Melbourne without visiting their parents has a car accident. Your logic astounds me."

"Vell, neverr mind about zat ..."

"No, never mind about that."

We talked for a while longer and she put me on to Dad.

"I'm glad you're okay, luv."

"Thanks, Dad," I said, feeling myself relax instantly.

We talked a bit more before he put Mum back on. I'd forgotten to ask about money. But I had to. There was no-one else. I bit the bullet and asked Mum instead. That was a mistake.

"Goot greeef!" Her accent had gone through the roof now. "Vot arr you talking about? My Gott!"

"Mum!"

"Vot iss it, do you sink ve are made off money? It iss ridiculous!"

"It's not ridiculous, it's a question and I need to know the answer. Where we live you need a car to get around. Who else can I ask? It's not like I'm leaving the country or something. Don't you think I'm good for it?"

She refused to go there. Instead she said, "Vell, I donn't make ze decisions about money in zis house. Your father duss zat, so you can talk to him about it." Muttering, she put down the phone and got Dad.

"Yes, luv. Of course I trust you to pay us back."

"Mum doesn't seem to."

"Don't listen to her; you know what she's like."

They were chalk and cheese. Opposites attract, they say. It was certainly true in this case. Dad would send me a cheque for two thousand dollars, to be paid back as and when I was able. No fuss. No distrust. No judgement. No *'eet – ees – reedeeculous'*.

Chalk and cheese.

Stella had a tall, wiry, tattooed brother who knew about cars. We were in South Melbourne looking at a Kingswood. She and I stood on the footpath watching seagulls and waiting for the verdict as the two blokes, heads under the bonnet, talked engines and mileage. I told Stella about the conversation with Mum.

"You should have heard the way she went on, like I was asking for the house and contents. It's not like they haven't got it. I wouldn't have asked if I thought it would leave them in a bad position."

"She gets a bit overwrought sometimes, doesn't she?"

"She drives me crazy."

"I'm glad your father didn't let her convince him not to lend you the money."

"I reckon. Thank goodness one of them is sane."

Her brother Brian came over to us.

"It's in good nick. It's in very good nick," he emphasised. "Buy it."

"That was really nice of Grandma and Grandpa to lend you money to buy a car," said Finn, as we got into our metallic-brown Kingswood.

"Sure was. You got your lunch?"

"Yep."

The green arrow to turn right on our one set of traffic lights in town came on. It must have been about a quarter to nine. I dropped him off at school. He closed the door, I waved and drove away.

Next thing I knew, I was parked on the other side of town outside a property belonging to a couple I had once rented from. I had no reason to be there and no recollection of having driven there. The ignition was off, the handbrake on, the car parked on the correct side of the road.

I sat for a long time until eventually it occurred to me I should go home.

As I pulled up in front of my house, I saw Emma sitting on the front porch. She had said she would come over for a coffee that morning. It was only when I saw her sitting there that I remembered. She could see there was something wrong and tried to make light of it as she came down the stairs, but the look of grave concern on her face gave her away.

"I'm sorry …"

"Forget it. What's wrong? You look like you've had a hard night on the town or something."

"Ha! Not likely. I don't know what's wrong. I dropped Finn off at school. Next thing, I'm sitting outside Tom and Kathy's house in a daze." I was as tired as I'd ever felt. "God I'm tired, and I only got up an hour ago."

"You should go to the doctor." I could hear the concern in her voice. "Those turns are coming back; but just by looking at you I can see this was much worse. Did you hit your head in that accident you had?"

"Yes."

"Shit. Go see the doctor."

"What do you think it is?"

"No, no, I'm not a doctor, I'm not gonna …"

"It's okay, tell me! What do you think it is?"

"I don't want to worry you," she said haltingly, "but I had a friend in Swan Hill who had epilepsy. He'd be just like you are now after he had a fit. You used to look out of it after one of those turns. But this is something else again."

"Jesus." That sinking feeling came over me. Epilepsy … There was that word again.

"But that was him. This might not have anything to do with epilepsy. Go to the doctor."

A few nights later Carol was over for dinner.

"Did you see the doctor today?"

"Yep."

"What did he say?"

"That what I was describing didn't sound serious, and until we get more information there's not a lot he can do."

"Hmmm." She didn't sound impressed. "What else did he say?"

"That I worry too much. That I should lighten up. And I don't think he meant lose weight."

"Lighten up. Your doctor seems to like that phrase, doesn't he?" She tried unsuccessfully to stop the annoyance coming through in her voice. "Get a second opinion."

"I intend to." I went over to the desk. "By the way, today I found this in the jacket I was wearing when I had the accident." It was a piece of paper they'd given me at the hospital when they discharged me.

"Look." I indicated one of the points on the list of recommendations. It read, *'Do not drink alcohol for at least 48 hours after a severe head trauma.'* "I forgot they even gave it to me."

"You mean you didn't read it?"

"No, I didn't. I mean … I might have," I hesitated. "But if I did, I forgot what it said. I didn't even remember calling Greg from the hospital to come and get me."

"And when they discharged you, you put that piece of paper in your pocket and forgot about it? Because you'd just hit your head and didn't even remember calling Greg?"

"Exactly. Then Lyn and I went out that weekend, when Finn was staying at Uncle Jim's. I didn't get drunk. Nowhere near it. I only had a glass of scotch and coke on a full stomach."

"But you think it might have been enough to upset your brain's recovery?"

"Maybe. Or maybe this was gonna happen no matter what I did …" I started to cry. "When I was in hospital, they only kept me there for a couple of hours. Oh Jesus, what have I done?"

"Mum, if you want to talk about it, I'll listen." I hadn't heard Finn come into the room.

We both gazed at him adoringly. I put my arms around him and wouldn't let go.

"You have to be the most gorgeous kid that ever lived, you know that?"

Carol agreed with me. "Yes. He's a very caring boy."

"He sure is." I dried the tears and asked him, "Have I been weird lately? It's okay to say 'yes' if I have."

"Yes, you have been a bit, Mum."

"Well, I'm going to find out what's going on. As soon as I know, I'll tell you what it is."

Electroencephalogram

"Mum?" Finn had come into the spare room at Uncle Jim's house. "We've been up for ages. Come and have some breakfast." Finn and I had stayed overnight. After seeing another doctor, I'd been booked in to have an electroencephalogram at Bendigo Hospital

"Morning. Oh … God …" I said, as I got out of bed. Why was I aching all over?

"You okay, Mum?"

"Not really, luv. I feel like I've got the 'flu or something. I didn't sleep much either."

"Uncle Jim said you were making funny noises last night. He was worried, so he came in to see what was wrong."

"What?"

"Don't you remember?"

"No," I said, squinting at the light from the kitchen window. Uncle Jim looked up from his bowl of cereal.

"It was about four in the morning," he told me. "You sounded like you were vomiting. So I went in to see what the matter was. I shook you awake. You opened your eyes, saw me and screamed. Then you went back to sleep."

I was incredulous. "What? Say that again?" I sat down at the kitchen table.

"You were making noises. I went in and shook you. You screamed and went back to sleep. You don't remember?"

"Not at all. What's happening to me?" Finn looked like he was about to cry. I knelt down and held him in my arms. "Whatever it is, I'll find out," I said, looking into his face. "Then, something can be done about it. Don't worry, darling." I felt like a hypocrite. I was scared stiff and telling him it was all okay.

"What time's your appointment?" my Uncle asked.

"Ten."

"Right. I'll drive you to the hospital. Leave Finn with me. I'll pack a few things and take him to your place. You get the train home after the tests are done. I'll stay at your place for a few days."

"It's okay, Mum. You'll be alright." I hugged Finn tighter. I had to find out what was happening to me. Leaving him in the world without his Mum was not on my agenda.

"We're going to stick these electrodes on your head."

Fabulous, I thought to myself.

"As you can see, they're attached to this machine. When we've got you all hooked up we'll turn it on and measure your brain's electrical activity," the technician informed me. "And this glue comes off with shampoo," she added.

"Good."

"Now, let's see what we can find out," she said as she turned it on.

The screen came alive with squiggly lines that dipped and rose. She observed it carefully.

"What do you think it is?" I asked after a while.

"I can't say that. It's up to the neurologist to diagnose you."

"Yeah, okay … But you must have some idea? From what you've seen before? I know you're not the doctor …"

"Well, from what I've seen before and from what's being recorded on the paper, it looks like epilepsy," she said. Once again she emphasised, "That's what it *looks like*."

"I shouldn't have asked."

"I can understand you being concerned. You'll find out for sure in the next few days, alright?"

"Thank you." I was looking forward to going home to 58 Green Street.

Uncle Jim was from a generation that made do with what they had. So now the unstable leg on our kitchen table had a bracket securing it, the door handle on the spare room actually shut the door and Finn had a new shelf in his room; and all in the space of half a day.

"Look at this, Mum." Finn was excited to show me as soon as I walked in.

"That's fantastic!" A piece of wood that had been in the shed was now attached to Finn's wall and painted red.

"Doesn't that look good, Mum?"

"Yeah, I'll say," I marvelled.

"We had some lunch, and he showed me a nest in the tree out there." Finn indicated the gum tree in the neighbour's garden. "He's having a nap."

"No I'm not." Uncle Jim came out of the spare room.

"Hi. The shelf in Finn's room is wonderful. Thank you."

"No problem. What did the doctor say?"

"Probably epilepsy. That's what she thinks it is. But it's not official yet. I have to see a specialist to find out for sure. She says there are different medicines you can take," I told them. "I've got to see a neurologist to find out which medicine suits me – if it's epilepsy …." I stroked Finn's cheek with my hand. "The main thing to remember is that it's treatable." I turned back to Uncle Jim. "Thanks for being here."

"That's fine," he said with a smile.

After dinner I left them to it and went to bed early. I wrote in my journal for a while then got out the Tarot cards, shuffled them, closed my eyes and picked two from the pack.

The Wheel of Fortune said: "*Augers a sudden change of fortune. This may be 'good' or 'bad'. But whichever way the wheel turns, it brings growth and a new phase of life. We cannot predict what will come to meet us, or rather what we will turn to meet. The Fool is thrown from his complacency and begins his descent into his own source.*"

The Five of Swords said: "*Augers the necessity of facing one's own limitations and recognising that life needs to be lived within the confines of one's own capabilities. Often there is a situation where the individual has taken on too much and must swallow pride and back off facing honestly what is possible before moving forward.*" Once again the cards had been spot on.

'Complacency' would no longer be an option; and as for 'living within the confines of one's capabilities', this 'fool' was about to get a rude awakening.

One of the new 'limitations' was the perfectly reasonable, but highly inconvenient, suspension of my driver's licence. This meant getting from our place to Mum and Dad's would take four hours instead of two. The last leg of the journey was a bus from Oakleigh station.

Growing up in Oakleigh had been your average existence in the Melbourne suburbs; safe enough back then. But things had changed in twenty years. At the back of the bus were six young guys, all teenage, loud, menacing and making a sound like hissing. The driver was a large man who would have no trouble scaring them into obedience. But I suspected even he would be intimidated by them if they decided to try anything. They were looking for trouble, or at least doing their best to make it sound that way. The security a car affords had been taken away. I hoped it was only temporary. I was looking forward to Mum and Dad making a fuss over me like they used to when I'd skinned my knee. I'd stay overnight at their house, then go to Brunswick where I was to meet the neurologist.

"*F*inn not viss you?" Mum asked, after we had all hugged.

"No. Carol is looking after him at her house."

"Who iss Carol? You leave your son viss a stranger? Oh, for God's sake, Anna, haven't you learned your lesson yet?" I'd only just put my bag down and it was 'on' already.

"Jesus Christ," I said (under my breath) as I made my way to the kitchen. Blasphemy was another of many things that was not tolerated.

"Slow down, Mum. Carol is no stranger. I've known her for years. She might be a stranger to you, but there's no way I'd leave Finn with someone I didn't trust," I said. "And because it's a weekday and I don't want him missing school. Chill out, everything's fine."

"Vell, I never know vott to expect viss you anymore."

"Nothing's going to happen to him, Mum. She's not going to capture him and take him to another country or something. Not like these people you watch every day on *Days of Our Lives*," I said as I gestured towards the television. She'd never missed an episode since they had bought their TV in 1969. On the screen, a man with a dimpled chin was arguing loudly with an extravagantly dressed woman. They looked angry enough to kill each other.

Dad added his voice to our debate. "Come on, luv, siddown. Mum's put the kettle on." His voice was gentle and soothing, his manner that of the peacemaker.

*D*r Elmore had glasses, a neatly trimmed beard and a businesslike manner. The tests had come back indicating that I did indeed have epilepsy.

"… as a result of head trauma from the accident," he told me. "Irregularities picked up on the EEG were conclusive evidence of epilepsy."

"Oh my God."

"So we'll start you on a course of Tegretol. Here's a script. It's extremely important you take them at the same time every day." He wrote the instructions on a piece of paper and handed it to me, along with the script. "Make an appointment to come and see me again in a month and we'll see how it's working. Also, you'll need to be booked in for an MRI."

"A what?"

"Magnetic Resonance Imagery. It will give us a clearer picture of where in your brain the epilepsy is coming from. The turns you told your GP about were epilepsy as well. Probably as a result of the accident you had in 1983."

"So all this is a result of that accident?"

"Yes. If you hadn't had the first one, it's unlikely you'd be having any of these troubles now."

"I see," I said with a sigh. "Hindsight is a fabulous and useless thing, isn't it?"

"Yes, you could say that."

"Will this ever go away?"

"Occasionally people find that their epilepsy symptoms change during the course of their lives. But in this case it doesn't seem likely," he said matter-of-factly.

I wondered if this was what it felt like when a judge in court banged the gavel down – life sentence, lock her up and throw away the key.

"There are a lot of things you'll have to do differently from now on. No alcohol. No late nights. No extreme stress – if you can avoid it, that is. And you'll need to maintain a blood level of anti-convulsant medication."

"Huh?"

"You have to take your medicine. It has to be taken every day if it's going to work. You need a certain level of it in your bloodstream at all times."

"Oh God …"

"It's better than the alternative." This fellow seemed a bit cold, as though he were on autopilot.

Or was I still in denial? I just wanted to get out of there.

*T*here's a scar on my brain, I thought to myself as I waited for the tram. The appointment was over, and Castlemaine was two hours by train.

Flickering lights trigger seizures in some epileptics, but not me. Strobe lights are okay, but alcohol's not. Temporal lobe epilepsy. Complex partial seizures.

The fresh air wasn't very fresh, but it was better than sitting in that office being told my whole life had to change.

How do they know that if I go out on a Saturday night I can dance under strobe lights but I can't have a drink? Not that I had any intention of arguing with them, even if it meant never touching another drop.

Take medicine for the rest of my life. What's this stuff he's put me on? What else does it do apart from stopping fits? I didn't want to think too much about that. Perhaps I'd just start walking. I could make it to the next tram stop before it got there.

When I got to the next stop, the Brunswick 96 tram still hadn't come.

Walk to the next one.

As I walked, I took in the fabric shops, cafes and fresh vegetable displays, the 7-Eleven that looked like all the others. I looked behind me. The tram still wasn't coming.

Walk to the next one.

A cafe had tables and chairs outside it. Crumbs under one set were being taken care of by sparrows. A bridal shop displayed exorbitantly expensive dresses. Still no tram.

Walk to the next one.

I walked to the next one and the next one. The tram I'd been waiting for passed me, but it didn't matter. The endorphins had kicked in. I gave myself a goal.

If I start feeling sorry for myself, I'm done for. I've got epilepsy, but I'm not in a wheelchair.

It took two hours to walk to Spencer Street station from Brunswick.

*I*n the supermarket, Emma saw me and called out.

"Anna!"

"Hey. Pension day."

"That's why I'm here too. Did you go and have those tests?"

"Yes. It's epilepsy."

"Oh, no way. I'm sorry."

"That's alright. It's not like you gave it to me or anything."

"So, what now?"

"Saw a specialist last week. I'm on this stuff called Tegretol."

"You feeling okay?"

"Yeah, no different."

"That's good."

"And I'm supposed to do all these things differently now. I have to turn the cold on in the shower first then the hot. I mustn't go swimming without someone with me. If I go walking in the bush, especially climbing in high areas, I should do the same. There are all these rules. And I can't drink alcohol any more either."

Emma gasped. "Anna!" she exclaimed, as she did her trying-not-to-laugh laugh.

"No more alcohol ever again. And I have to make sure I sleep properly. No more late nights. I don't have to be in bed before midnight, but I can't stay up till three in the morning, especially not for several nights in a row."

"What about driving?"

"No. Can't. I have to go three months without a fit before they let me anywhere near a car."

"Fair enough."

"God yeah."

After taking Tegretol for four months I had a fit at the gym. During an aerobics class I started talking to myself and staring into space. There was a mirror that ran the whole length of the wall we were facing. I walked towards it and left a print of myself on the mirror with the sweat produced by the work-out. When told this later, my extreme embarrassment prevented me from believing it.

So, clearly, Tegretol was not the right medicine for me. The specialist put me on Lamictal. Apart from stopping fits, this drug made some people feel like killing themselves. As well, life threatening skin rashes and moodiness were things to possibly look forward to. I couldn't wait.

A few more months went by. Although none of Lamictal's side-effects occurred in my case, the fits still happened sporadically, usually at full-moon and the day before a period. Hormones are a major catalyst for epileptic seizures. They can play a part in bringing on or controlling them. I was put on the pill as part of the treatment plan.

Different medicines were tried out on me, but just when I thought, *yes this one is working,* I would have another fit. The situation was far from ideal.

For Sale

It was almost two years since we'd moved into 58 Green Street. Finn had made friends at school and started playing soccer. Most of my friends had stayed with me, although one or two had fallen by the wayside. I wasn't fun to be around anymore if I couldn't stay out late on my weekends 'off' from mothering. Epilepsy continued to disrupt Finn's and my life. I kept reminding myself, it could be worse. Our real friends were supportive. We didn't have to move, and they knew where we were. One afternoon I came home to a message on the answering machine. It was from the landlord.

"Hello, it's George Pappas here. If the agent rings up about an inspection, make a time for them to come and have a look at the place. I'm thinking of selling."

Since when?

"No way," I said to no one in particular after I'd hung up the phone. I dried my eyes and blew my nose. Why was I reacting this way? Usually when we had to move again I'd just start packing.

The next house won't have brick walls you can't put pictures on, I would say to myself. *No more non-existent backyard. No more sleazy blokes or screaming kids. Hooray.* But there wasn't anything wrong with this place. Was this what it was like to feel at home? Just like the family had been hoping would happen all this time. So much for that.

Nobody wanted to buy it for the price they were asking. So, after months of having to keep the place spotless at all times, the For Sale sign was replaced by one saying Auction. On the day, a swarm of people would be poncing around the place all at once. I voiced my concerns.

"There'll be staff there all the time. You don't have to worry about anything going missing," the estate agent assured me. He was a nice guy, young and friendly. He understood my concern, but there was nothing he could do.

"Okay. I'm not happy about it, but it's the way it is I suppose."

"You don't have to be there on the day if it worries you."

"Oh, I'll be there. I'll be checking them all out and giving them the evil eye if they look suss."

He laughed but said, "I'd advise you not to give anyone the 'evil eye'. They could be the person who wants the place most. You might be putting them off. The sooner the place gets sold the better for you."

"That depends who buys it, doesn't it?" I wasn't in the mood to agree.

"What I mean is, at least then you'll know whether you have to move or not."

"Hmm. Yeah." I couldn't do a Clint Eastwood snarl, so I didn't try. He didn't deserve one anyway.

*O*ver dinner, Finn agreed with the estate agent's advice when I told him about our conversation.

"Don't do that Mum. It'll just make people feel weird."

"Yeah, I know. I wouldn't really. It's just this place ... well, it's so nice. Do you like it here?"

"Yeah, I do. And I don't want to move again."

"Me either. Will you be here that morning?" The auction was scheduled for the next Saturday.

"I don't know, Mum. Isaac might be having some friends over to sleep. I meant to ask you if I could go."

"Sure, luv. Now you have to help me with cleaning this place up. We have a week to make it spick-and-span."

"Oww, …" he objected.

"One hour a day. That's not much."

Between us we had cleaned every nook and cranny. They couldn't say we hadn't played our part. The sky was clear on the day which meant lots of potential buyers descended on our sanctuary. I sat on our porch watching them all. Around thirty people had come. A young fellow in suit and tie stood on the elevated section of the garden, looking like he was raring to go.

"We'll start the bidding at ninety thousand dollars. Do we have any takers?" A man at the back of the crowd raised his hand.

There was a woman in the front whose eyes were light blue with pupils like tiny dots. I wondered if she was on something. I'd never seen someone's pupils so small. She was looking intensely at the auctioneer, then over to the house and back to the auctioneer. She didn't blink.

"Ninety-one thousand? Do I have ninety-one?" She put her hand up. Acid rose in my stomach.

I hope she doesn't buy this house … I thought to myself … ambitious … greedy … raise the rent every year, get as much as she can out of us. Oh shit, she just bid again. Shut up and piss off, lady.

Things got competitive. There were several bidders interested. She bid again.

No, No, just go away, I don't want to move. Raze the house to the ground and start again, that's what you'll do. Build some hideous modern looking thing in its place. I can tell. You're the type. And your eyes make you look like you're on speed.

Not that I knew what someone's eyes looked like when they were on speed. But I had it in for this woman. My heart was in my mouth.

This was our home, and here she was about to destroy it all. *Don't buy this house ... don't buy this house ...* After a while, most of them stopped bidding. It was just her and the guy at the back. She bid again. The guy at the back didn't say anything.

"Anyone else?" The auctioneer could see it was over and so could I.

"Going once. Going twice. Sold, for ninety-five and a half thousand dollars." He hit his open hand with a rolled-up newspaper. "Congratulations," he told her.

They shook hands. I went inside to cry.

A few days later, I came home to find the unblinking speed woman in the backyard with someone else. They were measuring the boundaries of the property. I hadn't been told. I rang the agents.

"Is this what we can expect from now on? Just turning up whenever she feels like it? Or won't we be here to know?"

"Not so fast, not so fast," he said. "This is a one-off. The council requires measurements of the land before they'll grant her the title on the house. And she's not going to evict you, so you can stop worrying about that. You and your son can stay there as long as you want. It's an investment for her, okay?"

I burst out laughing. "Sorry, mate."

"That's okay," he said

I hung up the phone. The phone, the one in our house, the house with electricity, gas and beds to sleep in, a roof over our heads and somewhere to store our food. Our home. I had discovered what it was like to feel *at home*.

I made a toasted cheese sandwich. The griller was so old that tiny pieces of it sometimes fell onto what you were cooking. I lay down on the purple couch and flicked the black bits off into our lovely, homely fireplace that gave so much warmth and atmosphere. I placed cushions under my back so as to be in a semi-reclined position and ate my sandwich while looking at the marks on the ceiling (rats or possums occasionally crawled into the roof to die). I breathed another sigh of relief at not having to move from 58 Green Street.

Although the rent went up a few more times over the years, it remained one of the cheapest rental houses in town as property prices soared. She must have known what a good investment it was. No wonder she hadn't blinked until she'd secured the deal.

We never saw her again.

Epileptic Interference

One morning a week I went to Finn's school and read with the kids.

"How you going, Heather?"

"Good, and you?" his teacher replied.

"Yeah, alright, a bit tired this morning. Don't know why." Parents were encouraged to come and help out. Pictures adorned the walls – loving depictions of their dogs, cats and budgerigars. Others of cars and trains, and one of a stick figure person on what looked like a surfboard riding a wave. The rest of the page was coloured pastel blue to show the vast expanse of sea behind them. And there was one with 'Finn' at the bottom of it – a house, a tree and inside the house a woman with lots of frizzy red hair and a big smile on her face. She held something in her arms. It had a tail, four legs and was grey. Sheba.

Outside this house he had drawn faces that filled the rest of the page. Smiling faces, sad ones, cross-eyed ones, faces with a straight line for a mouth to indicate no particular emotion, faces with their mouths wide open.

I took this drawing to mean that there was the world outside and there was home, the place of sanctuary; I hoped that was how he felt.

I'd done everything I could to make it that way.

There were five kids in the group I read with. Finn was not one of them. That would have been too uncool. Even at this age his generation knew the rules of the game. It was like being teacher for an hour, holding up a book so they could see the pictures and read the words after me. All of a sudden, everything went weird; here was **The Feeling** again. I'd been here before. I was watching a replay of this scene. Time was going backwards. Then there was nothing. Then two women were guiding me down the hallway by my arms.

"Hey! What's going on?"

"It's alright, Anna. We're taking you to the staffroom to get you a cup of tea. You'll be fine."

"What's going on?"

"Come on, have a seat." It was Heather guiding me to a chair, her arm around my shoulder.

"What happened?"

"You had a turn, sweetheart. But you're okay now."

This epilepsy was like a monster following me wherever I went. "What happened this time? I mean, what did I do?" I asked. Apparently my eyes had rolled into the back of my head and I'd been dribbling.

"No way, did Finn see it?"

"Yes, but he handled it very well."

"Oh God …"

"He did, dear. Honestly. He realised what was happening before anyone else did. Saw you out of the corner of his eye and went straight over to you."

My licence kept being suspended every time I had another epileptic seizure. Depending on the severity of the fit, that meant one month or three. Uncle Jim had a car and took Finn off my hands occasionally, picking him up from our house.

"And another pair of socks. Put them in that side pocket," I said, "and that book you got? Where's that?"

"Packed it already," he told me. I recognised the car as it pulled up outside.

"Hello, you two," he called as he came up the steps.

"Hey," said Finn as they hugged.

"G'day, Finn. We're gonna pitch the tent in the backyard tonight, get some rocks, kindling, make a fire. Cook marshmallows, sausages, billy tea. How's that sound?"

"Sounds really cool." I breathed a sigh of relief listening to them talk.

"Cup of tea before you go?"

"I'd love one. What are you going to do for the next few days?"

I had found a washboard at a garage sale and made some gloves to play it with. I wanted to join a band, but the epilepsy made me unreliable, so I contented myself with going to jam sessions whenever I could.

"I'm going to go for a long bushwalk in the morning, and tonight there's going to be a jam session at the pub in town."

"Good. Hey, what about starting up a garden? You're a country girl now, going for walks in the bush and that; you've got a perfect little area here too," he said, gesturing to the front garden.

"But look at the soil. It's like a brick."

"If you don't water it, of course it is," he said matter-of-factly. I looked around. Our garden consisted of an apple tree and a half dead geranium. "Something your Aunt Lily taught me – the value of a garden. Your Dad likes his gardening too, doesn't he?

"Yes, he does."

When they drove away, I unravelled the ancient hose and turned it on for the first time since we'd been there. I had a flashback of Dad in his veggie garden, the hose in his hand, sometimes a smoke in the other. I remembered helping him in the garden, the pint-size wheelbarrow he had bought me. It was the smell that made me remember … of water and earth … the most beautiful smell in the world. A seed had been planted.

Red sky at night, sailor's delight; red sky in the morning, sailor's warning. Every time I saw pink clouds in the evening, I thought of that poem. The music session at the pub had started. I could hear them playing outside, but I was sitting just inside near the door, feeling odd, like I wasn't really present. As usual, I hadn't twigged why people were coming and checking on me all the time.

"You okay?" asked someone who had come up to where I was sitting.

"Yeah ... why?" I replied.

"How you going? You alright now?" said a friendly young fellow who had popped his head around the door just as a song ended.

"Why is everybody asking me that?" I must have sounded sharp. He went back outside again.

"Hey! Hold on, what's the matter? Why is everyone asking if I'm alright?" But he hadn't heard me.

Where was the nearest toilet? I suddenly needed to go urgently. (This is common after a fit.) As I got up from the bench, a woman rushed over.

"Where you going?"

"Toilet," I told her in vexed tones. It was as though she were trying to stop me. *She'd better think twice about that,* I thought.

"Do you want me to go there with you?"

This is getting weird. Why does she want to do that? "I can go there by myself, thanks. I'm fine. People keep asking me if I'm okay. Why?"

"Don't you know?" she asked as she walked beside me.

"Know *what*?" My stomach was urging me on to that toilet.

"We'd been practising for about ten minutes," she told me. "Then you just started walking away with this dazed expression on your face. You were talking to yourself and you went off towards the road. There was a car coming. Bob had to run and get you, or you'd have walked in front of it."

"*What?*"

"Didn't you know?"

"No!" She was clearly confused now, but even what she was telling me was not enough to distract me. "Listen, I've only got one thing on my mind right now, okay?"

She was waiting for me when I came out of the toilet, looking more concerned than before. "You alright?"

"Yes, I mean I feel a bit tired. But don't worry about that. What were you saying just now?"

"You walked that way. Then you veered that way," she said incredulously, pointing to where I'd apparently gone, "over there, where the cars are parked, and you looked like you were headed for the road. You don't remember?"

"No! I don't remember anything like that. You said Bob ran after me?"

"Yes. And you were talking to yourself. It was hard to understand what you were saying. Before all that, you were just playing with everyone. Then you started saying something nobody could understand, stopped playing the washboard and just started walking, staring into space."

It had happened again.

"When we got you over to the bench, you were sweating and confused."

"How long did it go for?"

"From the time you started talking to yourself till we sat you down on the bench? Two or three minutes."

"That's not possible! I don't believe it."

"But you're much better now. You're speaking English again and you're arguing the point," she said, trying to make light of the situation.

"No, I'm not."

"Yes, you are!"

"No, I'm not!"

It was nice that she was laughing *with* me not *at* me. God knows what I must have looked like, staring into space and talking in tongues.

"I might go home. Thank you for looking after me. I'll just get my stuff and say goodbye to everyone. Where's my washboard?"

"We put it over here," she said picking it up and handing it to me. "And your bag's over there. You came on your bike, didn't you? Are you sure you should ride home after that?"

"Yes, it's fine. I'm alright now."

"No, no, I don't want you doing that. Bob has his ute. You can put the bike in the back and he'll drive you home."

"I can't expect him to …"

"Yes, you *can*!"

Jesus, Mary and Joseph

Epilepsy invaded every aspect of my life. It put Finn and me on edge, as it seemed there was no solution to the problem. Doctors put me on different medications, but none of them worked. After the very clinical way Dr Elmore had told me about the possible side-effects of Lamictal, I asked my GP to find me another specialist. Dr Jenkins was a tall, softly spoken Buddhist man. Changing specialists wouldn't change my condition, but at least I would get some empathy.

I understood the need to stay off the road, but relying on other people to drive us around was embarrassing. I sometimes complained about the change in our lifestyle to friends and got various responses. Linda, a friend of Emma's, responded by offering to enlist the help of God.

She had been going to one of those churches where people collapse on the floor and writhe around. When she told me this had happened to her, I recommended my new neurologist. She was not inclined to make an appointment to see him. I came home one day to find sticks on the front porch. They had been arranged to spell out a message. It read: 'Jesus loves you'.

Since having 'seen the light', she felt a duty to reach out to me or anyone who was in any way receptive. She knew about the epilepsy.

I was not interested in religion, and she knew that too. Perhaps she genuinely believed she and her boyfriend could help. Perhaps she wanted to convert us. I suspected both.

I was coming to terms with the new her. As long as she didn't think epilepsy was a manifestation of satanic possession, I decided I could cope. Since Uncle Jim had convinced me to take up gardening, I also wondered what God would think about all the apples that wouldn't get a chance to grow because of the branches she'd taken off our tree. She called me a few days later offering help from the Lord in the form of a hands-on healing.

"Yeah, okay, see you then. Bye." I hung up and told Finn, "Linda's coming over after dinner tonight."

"Isn't she coming over for tea as well?"

"No, she's just coming over for a little while, to give me a hands-on healing."

"What's that?" he said in a tone of childlike scepticism.

"Well ..." How would I explain? "You know how she believes in God these days?"

"Yeah?"

"Well she wants to see if God can help me with this epilepsy," I explained.

"But she's not God." Children are the wisest of all.

"Uh, no ..." I said suppressing the urge to laugh, "No, she's not."

"Does she think she is?" He was starting to get worried now. He'd met some of my more eccentric hippie friends in Melbourne.

"No, she doesn't, luv." I was trying to be serious. "No, she, um..." What *was* she on about? "She believes, because she goes to church and prays to Jesus, that she has a connection with him. And because of that he can help people; through her."

Finn rolled his eyes.

"You never know, you never know. Something good might come of it," I said.

"Yeah, sure, Mum." He didn't sound convinced.

*A*t eight o'clock, there was a knock at the door. Linda, effervescent as usual, walked down the hallway with her boyfriend Richard.

"Hi, how are you? Finished dinner?"

"Yep. Dishes still in the sink, but that's nothing new," I said.

She laughed her bubbly laugh and gave Finn a hug as she came into the lounge room. Richard followed silently behind. He was one of those unassuming types.

"How was school?"

"Okay," Finn said.

"Great!" She wanted him to say it was wonderful, because everything was wonderful to Linda. Especially now that she'd found God.

"Sit down and I'll make us a cuppa," I said. "Or will we have one later?"

"I might even have to make *you* one later. The power of God might be so strong within you that you'll need to just sit down and rest," she said exuberantly.

"Yeah, maybe," I said, hoping the scepticism wasn't showing. Wouldn't the power of God energise me rather than zap me? Give me enough get-up-and-go to make tea, scones, cake, tomorrow's dinner and clean the whole house before bedtime? I didn't press the issue. Instead I said, "Okay, I'll lie down over here, will I?"

"Yes, wherever you're comfortable, Anna. Just relax and let the Lord do his work."

I did as instructed and lay on my stomach in front of the fireplace. For the next half an hour she and Richard placed their hands on my back, shoulders and head, praying, absorbing the goodness of God and hoping I would do the same. Their faith was quite sincere.

Next day I was sweeping the front porch. When The Feeling started, I went and sat in an armchair. Betty next door happened to come outside shortly afterwards to find me staring into space, talking gibberish and rocking myself. The power of the Lord had not helped the sinner. I did not mind.

A few weeks later, Linda was still exuberant about God. We bumped into each other in the street.

"I'm saying spirituality is important to me, but I'm not interested in religion. If finding God has made you happy, I'm glad for you. It's just not for me."

She looked disappointed, but I wasn't going to be swayed. She'd been trying to convert me ever since she'd had her revelation.

"Well, I'm sorry to have bothered you about it, Anna. If you ever change your mind and want to come to one of our services, you need only ask and we can go there together."

I could have said, don't hold your breath, but that would only have driven another nail into the coffin our friendship seemed to be in these days.

"Thank you. I've got to go do some shopping now. I'll seeya, Linda." I doubted I would. Not only was she totally hooked, she needed her friends to believe the same as she did, or that was the end of that.

*A*s for Finn, he very sensibly relied on his own resources instead of those of Jesus. I was sure The Man Himself, having been a carpenter, would appreciate Finn's practical bent. Much as I'm sure Finn would have loved to heal me instantly if he could, he had instead invented a strategy for occasions when I took fits.

It was a Saturday morning. We were going to the market to get vegetables. But there was something else we had to do as well, and I couldn't remember what it was. My diary was on the kitchen table. I would look at it as soon as I got myself some breakfast. With a bowl of cereal in one hand I was opening the fridge with the other. I started having The Feeling and went down 'like a ton of bricks', as Dad would've said. The bowl and cereal went everywhere as I fell. Next thing I knew, I was on the purple couch, Finn next to me. He had his arm around my shoulders and was asking me something.

"Who are you? Who am I?" It sounded like such a reasonable question. But I couldn't answer it. I was rocking myself.

"Huh?"

"Who are you? Who am I?" he repeated in a composed voice.

I looked at him blankly.

"Who are you? Who am I? You had a fit, Mum."

"No I didn't!" I replied instantly. My unwillingness to believe it was proof that, somewhere in my mind, I knew exactly what had happened.

"Yes you did, Mum."

"No, I didn't." I kept up the denial a while longer.

On the lounge room floor were the latest craze toys, Ninja Turtles, abandoned in favour of rescuing his mother from herself. He had changed roles, taken charge instantly and with ease. On the kitchen floor were cereal and broken pieces of crockery.

"Who are you? Who am I?"

"Anna McAllister," I answered robotically as I rocked myself.

"That's right, Mum," he said encouragingly like his school teacher. "And who am I?"

"Finn. Finn McAllister."

"That's right, Mum. And who is this?" Sheba was flouncing elegantly towards us, meowing as if she knew there was something wrong.

"Sheba." I reached for her and she snuggled onto my lap. Her fur was soothing to the touch. She started to purr.

Later that day, I was defrosting the fridge and was pleased to get a huge square slab of ice out of the freezer using a hammer and chisel. Just then, my little boy walked into the room. Seeing the result of my work, he realised the opportunity in front of him. His eyes lit up.

"Can I break it, Mum?!"

I handed him the large piece of ice. "Of course you can!" He took it into the backyard and smashed it on the concrete; one of the truly simple pleasures of life. He was immensely satisfied with the result. So was I. It was much better than having to morph into a nurse at the drop of a hat when you were only eight years old.

A few weeks later, Linda and I were on my porch steps having a cup of tea. It was a cool, almost cold day that was looking like rain.

"This church I've been going to has challenged many of my beliefs and feelings," she said, "but it's something that feels right for me at this time in my life, so I'm going to keep going."

"I see. So, you're telling me this for a reason, aren't you? It sounds that way," I said.

"There is something, yes. I don't quite know how to say it. The church …" she hesitated, then went on, "requires you to adhere to a set of rules and commitments. One is that you cut ties with anyone you know who is not involved with it."

Was she saying what I thought she was saying? And in such a matter-of-fact voice, like someone from social security telling you your payment had stopped.

"You've got to be kidding. Because I don't believe in God, you aren't going to have anything to do with me anymore? Or Finn? That's totally fucked. That's not …"

"Anna, it pains me to say it, but it's something I have to do. I want to bring Adrian up in an environment where he doesn't have to worry about …"

"About what? What kind of people do you think we are? Psychos? Take a look around you. There are plenty of people your kids shouldn't associate with, even in this town. But that does *not* include Finn and me!"

Linda and Richard were parents like I was. They, in their way, were trying to provide the best environment for their son. That was something I had no trouble understanding. But for the life of me, I couldn't see why she was being asked to turn her back on her friends. I didn't think Jesus would like it either. But there it was, religious fanaticism had struck again.

"Look, I'm sorry, but …"

"You already said that. If God is telling you not to be here, then why are you still here? Seeya."

As soon as he got home, Finn could see I'd been crying.

"What's wrong, Mum?"

"Linda says she doesn't want a friendship with me anymore. Because of that church she's been going to."

There was empathy in his eyes that stunned me. I didn't know why it should, but it did. As he hugged me, I realised once again just how capable children are at caring for others. You hear kids being talked about in uncomplimentary ways all the time; 'spoilt brat', 'bully', 'selfish', etc. But what did you ever hear about their capacity for wisdom and compassion? It seemed to me at that moment that a lot of kids were more like Jesus than the adults who told you Jesus loved you.

Taking Leave of My Senses

Something I'd noticed since becoming a sole parent was the attitude of married/partnered women. As a single mother, I found it hard to make conversation with men who were spoken for, not because I had nothing to say, but because their partners would often whisk them away. It's not like I was some kind of 'sex-bomb'. I was an ex-hippie who hadn't made a point of getting my abs or anything else back into shape after giving birth. But just knowing I was single, and therefore (supposedly) a threat, was reason enough, it seemed. No words were needed. A cold-as-ice vibe in the air was enough. It's a female thing. In times past I'd probably done it myself.

Even if you'd never dream of going near someone unavailable, it made no difference. The unspoken assumption was that, if you were 'alone', you were desperate not to be. Which meant you might cross boundaries you shouldn't. I didn't. Even so, most of my friends were single or sole parents. Thankfully, Finn was making friends with kids from various family backgrounds. His mates did not seem to care whether his Mum was single or not. I believed this went further to prove the theory.

Linda had become bewitched by extremist Christians, which meant one less friend to hang out with. But they say when one door closes another opens. Ben and Lisa had moved in across the road from us. We'd become friends instantly.

An 'alternative' couple, they didn't fit the mould. Lisa was just alternative. But Ben was having an alternative to his alternative. He was gay but had fallen in love with Lisa, which was something he had not expected.

At the end of our street was a bushland reserve. Finn and I walked there often. Ben and Lisa were keen on nature and had started walking with us. The Saturday market was two hour's walk there and back. We had gone there and arrived home laden with vegetables, exhausted but satisfied. "Come and have some lunch," I suggested.

Sitting in a bean bag, drinking coffee with friends and enjoying the natural high from a long walk filled me with contentment.

The Feeling came over me as I took my first sip. I had just enough time to put my cup on the floor.

Once I was all right again, Ben was eager to tell me what I had been doing during the fit. It sounded like I'd added a bit of variety to my usual act this time; an alternative to my alternative.

"You were rolling a cigarette," he told me.

"You're kidding." This was more bizarre than usual.

"You were rolling a smoke!"

"It was pretty funny, Mum," Finn said.

"I don't smoke. Not for a long time," I said.

"While you were having that fit you looked like you were rolling a cigarette. You got a paper out of a packet," he said, making corresponding gestures. "Then you reached for another packet. That must have been the tobacco. You dipped into it, put some 'tobacco' onto the 'paper' and rolled it. You even brushed some off your leg where you'd spilt some."

I laughed incredulously. "Did I light it?"

"No, you stopped rolling your smoke then and started talking in another language."

"Oh right. Of course I did." Nothing surprised me anymore. "What's it gonna be next time ... a strip show?"

"The full monty!" suggested Ben. We laughed uproariously.

Instead of giving me the ice-cold vibe at that point, Lisa looked at my cup of coffee, which had gone cold, and asked, "Now that you're feeling more like yourself again, would you like me to make you another cup of coffee to go with your 'cigarette'?"

"Thank you, that would be lovely."

"Muuuuuwww." Sheba was glad I was better again, too. She jumped onto my lap.

*F*it stories were good conversation pieces. I had plenty of them to tell. After three years, Finn and I had learned to accept them as part of our life. But I was supposed to be looking after him, not the other way around. I resented what epilepsy did to me as a mother. I was telling Jenny, a friend who lived in Melbourne, about how hormones played havoc with my brain.

"Premenstrual tension has turned into something more sinister than it usually is, especially when it coincides with a full moon."

"It makes you sound like a vampire or something," she said.

"Vot doo yoo mean *sound* like?" I responded, using Mum's accent.

"Ha! So, how often do you have fits? Is it just that time of month or other times as well?"

"Mostly around PMT time and full moon, but it's not restricted to those times. Just when it seems like they've found the right medicine for me, I have another fit. They're trying me on another drug now, but you have to come off the old one, and doing that can cause fits as well." Topamax was the latest one not to have worked. It was a relief to be coming off it. "Anti-convulsants sometimes interfere with emotions. Since I started taking Topamax, I've had a feeling something isn't right. Like I've been on the edge of some emotional hole and if I fall into it I'm going to be in big trouble." As I tried to describe my state of mind, I wondered if I was explaining it properly.

"I know someone else with epilepsy," said Jenny. "He says the same thing. He wonders if having a mental illness is similar to the way he feels on some of the medications they've tried him on."

"I think I understand." It seemed everyone knew someone with epilepsy.

"Well, I'm glad you're coming off … what's it called?"

"Topamax. Yes, me too. So if Saturday's okay I'll take the train in and be at your place about five. Is that okay?"

"Sounds good. It'll be nice to catch up." We hung up.

Uncle Jim had Finn that coming weekend. I would take the train to Melbourne. Once I got there, I would meet Greg for a coffee in the city, visit Stella in North Melbourne and then go to Jenny's in Fitzroy and stay overnight.

Flinders Street station under the clocks, one of the main meeting spots in the Melbourne CBD, was where my cousin and I had arranged to meet. People stood around checking their watches or looking into the distance for whoever they were waiting for. It was a relief to sit and be somewhere else besides Castlemaine, watching the constant stream of people, strangers rushing to and fro. A broad-shouldered man, who looked to be at least six-foot-six, was walking up the steps nearby. He was extremely good looking.

"Anna, don't perve on strange men," said Greg cheekily in my ear. I jumped, my heart rate having instantly doubled.

"Where the hell did you come from? You scared the crap out of me."

"I thought it best. What if he turned around and saw you?"

"That's a bad thing? He was stunning," I said as we stood up to walk.

"Can't really see it myself," he said wryly.

"Just believe me, okay. How about that coffee," I suggested in an attempt to change the subject. "Why don't we get take-aways, come back here and sit on the steps?"

"So you can find more men to perve on?"

I made a face at him.

"I have to be back at work in half an hour. But then I won't be working for 'em much longer, so it won't matter if I'm ten minutes late," he told me as we went in search of coffee.

"Oh?"

"I quit. Found another job. Fuck, I hate these things," he said, loosening his tie.

"Why did you quit?"

"They're underpaying me, so I got a job with their rivals. They're not happy," he said with satisfaction.

When we got back to the steps at Flinders Street, a young guy with a twelve-string guitar was singing *Bobby McGee*. "That sounds better than the original," I said, recalling Janis Joplin's raspy version.

"Remember that guy in the wheelchair who used to busk there playing the bagpipes?" Greg asked me, pointing to where the guy was standing.

"Yes, I used to see him almost every day when I conducted the trams," I told him.

"One day I saw him stand up, fold up his wheelchair and walk away," he told me with amusement.

I looked at him, dumbfounded. "Is nothing sacred?"

"Sorry to burst your bubble, Anna, but no," he replied, taking another sip of his coffee.

After Greg and I said goodbye, I got on a tram to Bourke Street. Young girls sat trying to look perfect. Young guys huddled in groups talking, probably about the girls. The older men and women looked serious in comparison.

The Feeling came over me just before Collins Street. Last thing I remember was an old Greek-looking man in a suit and tie standing up to get off.

"'Scuse me, luv," he said. What happened from then on is pure speculation.

People on the tram were most likely taken aback by my behaviour as I started to fit. That would probably have taken the form of incomprehensible speech, rocking back and forth, my eyes rolling into the back of my head or a blank facial expression.

The young guys may have laughed at the freak show taking place a few meters away. I can imagine what their conversation might have turned to:

"*What's she on?*"

"*Dunno, but I don't want any ...*"

"*Does smack do that to you?*"

"*Not sure. I think she's just loopy.*"

The young girls must have thought I was *extremely* imperfect. This would have shown on their flawless faces as embarrassment, unease and discomfort.

Or perhaps the Greek-looking man had seen me just in time and stayed next to me for a few more stops, chastising the younger ones for their lack of concern? Or maybe the young ones were compassionate individuals.

"*Is she having a fit?*"

"*Think so. Hey! Hello, you alright?*" moving his hand in front of my face, snapping his fingers. "*She's not responding.*"

"*Yeah that's a fit. Charlie does this when he has one.*" Perhaps they gathered around me and looked after me. I'll never know. I was only semi-present. By the time I became *compos mentis*, we were at the terminus in Carlton, way past Bourke Street. Nobody was offering me help, but no-one had stolen my bag either. Perhaps the spectacle hadn't even registered for most of them, just another day in the Melbourne CBD, just another space-case regressing back to infancy.

The driver ushered me over to a bench. "You can get a taxi from here. But you just sit for a while, okay? Don't go anywhere till you feel alright again."

"Thank you. I won't go anywhere. I just need to sit for a bit."

"You take care," he said in a voice that sounded genuinely concerned. He had a tram to drive. He had to go.

I sat for a while, trying to remember where Stella lived and how you got there. She had lived in North Melbourne as long as I'd known her, which was a long time. Jenny, on the other hand, had only just moved to her flat in Fitzroy, so thankfully I had written the address down. I would have to go straight there and contact Stella when I could remember her number.

"How much is it to get to Fitzroy?"

"About ten bucks," replied the taxi driver, 'about' being the operative word. "Where we going? I need a street."

"Yes, yes, of course."

"You're early," said Jenny opening her door.

"Change of plan, had a fit on the tram."

"Oh no." She hugged me tightly.

"It's such a pain," I said wearily. Then I remembered. "I have to call Stella. She'll be wondering where I am."

"There's the phone," she said, pointing to the bay window sill. Only trouble was, I still couldn't remember her number. It was so familiar to me I hadn't bothered writing it anywhere. It was like I'd never known it at all.

"Maybe someone on that what-number-are-you-looking-for line can give it to me."

"What phone number are you enquiring about?"

"Stella Smith. She lives in North Melbourne." I realised instantly how stupid it sounded.

"That's a very common name," she said tersely.

"I don't remember her address." I should have hung up then. But I literally didn't have the presence of mind.

"Well, I need an address."

"Oh God, I don't remember it, but I need to call her ... Oh forget it." Then I remembered, "The name of the street starts with A ... that's right, starts with the letter A."

That was still not enough. "Well, I'm sorry I can't help you if you can't be more specific," she said as though I were a recalcitrant child.

"Yeah, okay. Bye."

"That went well," observed Jenny.

"Yeah, it did, didn't it? Stella, I've called her a million times. How could I not remember her number?"

"You just had a fit. Don't be so hard on yourself. I've got some shopping to do. Why don't you go and have a sleep? Your bed's made up."

"You're a treasure," I told her.

Outside, a tram driver was ringing insistently on his bell. Someone must have done something stupid. The doona around me was comforting. Sleep came easily.

When Jenny got back, we went to get some dinner. Jenny's second-storey flat looked out onto tram cables. The flat across the road had rainbow scarves and a Buddha in the window. The shop underneath it was a health cafe. We found a table with comfortable chairs.

"You look better than when you arrived today. So what happened?"

"I felt absolutely fine all day. Then the deja vu feeling came over me when I was on the tram, just before Collins Street. Then I ... took leave of my senses. Next thing I knew, I was in Carlton. I can't tell you much more than that."

"And everything in between is a blank?"

"Yep. Everything."

"I don't know how I'd cope if I had epilepsy. I'd be too scared to go anywhere."

"The fit's not the scary part. You're out to it then. It's everybody else who's freaking out when that's happening. But then, afterwards, you feel so helpless. The tram driver just took me to a bench and left me there. He didn't like doing it, but he had to keep to his timetable."

"You didn't look the best, even once you got to my place."

"Sometimes people don't realise," I told her. "They think you're fully recovered just because you can put a sentence together in English again. But your mind's a blank after a fit for a long time, hours, even days."

"I can imagine."

"Oh … I don't think you can, Jen. It's not like a hangover or something."

She looked at me without saying a word, one eyebrow arched.

"I don't mean you get hangovers all the time," I reassured her. "Actually, I was remembering the ones *I* used to get."

"You and me both," she said reminiscently. "Remember the night we all went to the Pink Floyd gig and went to my place after that?"

"How could I forget?" I said with embarrassment. "Let me rephrase that. More like, how come I remember any of it?"

She laughed, no doubt remembering the state I'd been in when I woke up on her couch next morning all those years ago.

"What I mean about hangovers is, you wake up feeling awful, but you know why you feel that way, and you take a tablet."

"And a hair of the …"

"… dog that bit you? Never done that! But after a fit, it's like there's nothing going on in your mind at all. And there's nothing you can do about it. You literally can't think. Somebody asks you the simplest question, and you can't answer it."

"Like when you were trying to get Stella's number?"

"Yeah. I drew a total blank. It just wasn't in there," I said, pointing to my head. "It's the same when Finn's there after I have a fit. He asks me, 'Who are you? Who am I?' I can't even tell him that until he's asked me about fifty times."

"Do you know why you're having fits again this time?"

"The doctors are trying me on another medicine. But I'm still coming off the last one. It's always like this. It's withdrawal. Remember I was telling you on the phone?"

"Yes."

"But this time I've been doing lots of reading – 'know your enemy' and all that. There's something called neuroplasticity."

"Yes, I've heard of it."

"I'm sure it's more complicated than this, but they say actual physical 'pathways' are formed in the brain. Just like a track in the bush."

"Pathways?"

"Yes. Not visible to the naked eye of course. You know how if someone thinks the same way for long enough it gets harder to change the thought if they want to? That's an example of an established pathway in the brain."

"You get set in your ways?"

"Exactly. Same thing if you take a medication regularly and for long enough. You develop dependency on it which is visible, by means of a microscope or whatever, as a neurological pathway."

"You've slept off that fit, haven't you?" she said with an amused grin. "So, based on that theory the same could be said for addictions? Someone gets hooked on something which shows up as a pathway in the brain?"

"Yes. So I guess I'm withdrawing from drugs ..." I said, looking up and seeing a gorgeous guy standing at our table ready to take our orders. "Legal ones," I said hastily. "Prescribed by a doctor," I added, looking at Jenny sheepishly.

He smiled and laughed. We ordered vegetarian stir-fry and rice. He was dark and broad-shouldered with dreadlocks. We both checked him out as he walked away.

"So they've put me on something called Dilantin," I told her. "My specialist thinks this one will work."

A week later, I was on the phone to someone from the Epilepsy Foundation. My specialist, Dr Jenkins, was fairly confident that the latest drug, Dilantin, was the one for me. But I was still in withdrawal from my last medication, Topamax. To help compensate for this, my GP had increased the Dilantin from 500 to 700mg. I was a zombie.

"That does sound rather high," the man from the Foundation said.

Beyond that he wasn't prepared to comment.

"It feels like too much. I can't think straight. You know how it is when you get up in the morning and you need time to wake up? I go through the whole day feeling like that. It's like I'm only half here."

"I do understand. But I'm not allowed to give medical advice. I recommend you call your specialist and ask him what he thinks. Perhaps he will recommend a slightly lower dose that deals with the fits and leaves you feeling a bit brighter."

"Yes, thank you, I'll do that."

Doctor Jenkins was surprised the dose had been increased so much at once, not to mention the fact that he had not been told. But, as usual, he sounded calm and composed.

"No, Anna, that's much too high. Six hundred milligrams should make quite enough difference; it's just the occasional fit breaking through. An extra hundred ought to keep them at bay. Go down to six hundred, and I will let your doctor know as well."

But six hundred milligrams wasn't enough after all. There seemed to be only two choices left for me: go back up to seven hundred or go under the knife.

Attention All Visitors

*I*t was one of those things you never dream you will say.

"Please let me have brain surgery," I begged, tearfully. "Everything's a mess. I can't plan anything because I never know when the next fit's coming." It had been four years since I'd gotten epilepsy, and what they called 'breakthrough seizures' were still happening. Dilantin was the best so far, but no drug worked completely.

Dr Jenkins sat at his desk listening as I poured out my concerns, hands together in front of him, fingertips touching.

"I'm scared something's going to happen, something that will put Finn in danger, or me. I'm trying to be a good mother, just trying to live my life, for God's sake …" He must have heard patients say this kind of thing constantly. I'm sure he was getting paid very well to do it, but he did seem genuinely concerned. The possibility of surgery if medicines failed was something he'd mentioned before.

"It's looking more and more as though surgery might be the best option," he said.

"Really?" I said, sitting up straighter.

"Needless to say, surgery isn't something we do at the drop of a hat. There has to be good reason to perform an operation of that magnitude," he said. "But tablets on their own don't seem to be enough to keep your seizures at bay. If scar tissue on your brain from the accident has given you epilepsy, then taking away as much of that tissue as possible could give you control over the seizures."

"What a blessing that would be. How does scar tissue cause fits?" I asked.

"By interrupting brain activity," he replied.

"How come interrupted brain waves make you have a fit?"

"We don't know exactly what causes epileptic seizures," he said in the same measured way.

I blinked. Had I heard him correctly? Hadn't he just told me what caused them? This guy was a neurologist with a string of letters after his name. If there was something to know about epilepsy, he knew it. *It would take too long to explain,* I decided.

"There are tests we can do to measure emissions of positrons from your brain cells."

"Groovy," I said in an impressed tone. Positrons. I didn't know what they were, but it sounded good.

He smiled. "It's groovy, alright," he said in his most scholarly voice. "Tests can help us determine whether or not brain surgery is a viable option. The scar tissue may be located in an area in the brain that can't be reached without severely risking normal functions, in which case, surgery would not be recommended. But," he added "if we found there was a reasonable chance of achieving something without making things worse, we would then have you undergo a series of assessments to prepare you for surgery."

All of a sudden, there was light at the end of the tunnel.

*F*inn looked as though he was impressed, relieved, scared and surprised, all at the same time.

"Brain surgery, Mum?"

I instinctively reached out for him. How could I just stand idle while he stood there, experiencing all those emotions at once?

"Yep, that's what he told me. It's not definite yet. But wouldn't that be something?"

"It sure would, Mum." He put his arms around me.

If I got scared about it, all I had to do was remember the other person besides me who needed this to happen.

A few days later, Dad seemed to be deep in thought at their kitchen table. He was trying to accept the idea of his little girl having her skull opened.

"Well, Anna, that's really something; brain surgery. A bloke at work has a nephew who had an operation for his epilepsy. He told me how this boy had to wear a helmet all the time because he had it so bad. After he had the operation, he was a new person." He put his arm around my shoulder.

"Oh my Gott." Mum had her hands resting on her mouth and looked skywards for a moment. "When are they going to operate on you?"

"I don't know if they will or not. I've got to be induced to have a fit in hospital so they can read my brain waves or something." Mum cringed.

"What does that mean?" Dad wanted to know.

"They will make me have a fit by reducing my medicine. In the hospital. A safe environment where they can look after you when it happens. Then they can also see where in the brain the fits are coming from." I held Mum's hand and squeezed it. "It'll be fine, Mum. It's the Austin Hospital. They have the best neurology department in the Southern Hemisphere."

Finn was sitting on the floor watching TV.

"What do you think about your Mum having brain surgery?" Dad wanted to know.

"It's cool, Grandpa. I hope it happens soon so Mum can stop having fits."

"So, why do they have to make you have a fit before they can operate on you?" Mum wanted to know.

"Scar tissue from the accident is what causes the fits. Or it probably is. That's what they're trying to find out. The fits come from the same places in the brain each time. The idea is to get rid of as much of the scar tissue as possible. But they have to make sure that when they take the scar tissue away, they don't take out bits of my brain as well." Mum looked skywards again as if praying to God. "I know, it sounds awful. It *is* awful. I'm trying not to think too much about it either, or I'll chicken out. But, like I said, it's the Austin Hospital. They really know their stuff." *Christ, I hope they do,* I thought to myself. Mum and I kept holding hands for a while longer before she put the kettle on the stove.

"Mum, you've had that kettle for thirty years. Don't you think it's time you got another one?"

"No, iss perfectly alright," she said dismissively.

ATTENTION ALL VISITORS:
A RADIOACTIVE COMPOUND HAS BEEN INJECTED INTO THIS PATIENT FOR SCANNING PURPOSES. IT IS SUGGESTED THAT YOU SPEND AS LITTLE TIME AS POSSIBLE IN CLOSE PROXIMITY TO THE PATIENT FOR THE FIRST TWELVE HOURS AFTER THE INJECTION.
NOTE: PREGNANT WOMEN AND CHILDREN SHOULD AVOID CONTACT WITH THE PATIENT FOR 24 HOURS.

The notice on the end of my bed was less than reassuring. As long as people stayed away from me, they were safe. But there was nowhere *I* could go. It was the Austin Hospital's neurology department. I had pieces of metal glued to my head, attached by cables to a machine. A screen showed my brain activity, while another machine printed it out constantly. The only place I was allowed to go was the toilet, and even then I had to ask for assistance to get there. It was like having an umbilical cord, and I felt like a helpless baby.

The amount of medicine I took was being reduced each day. They did this on purpose, to induce a fit while I was hooked up to the machinery, which would then record it. To have a fit here was a good thing.

Earlier that day, I had felt The Feeling. Before losing consciousness, I had pressed the emergency buzzer as I'd been instructed. What happened next is pure conjecture on my part – doctors and nurses rushed to my room, working as a team to get me and all the machinery to the MRI room as fast as they could, like they do on those Hospital Emergency shows. Once there, they would have injected me with the 'radioactive substance' which highlighted the areas of my brain where fits were coming from, and then put me in the Magnetic Resonance Imagery machine.

"Hello, Anna," said the nurse cheerily. "How are you feeling now?"

"Um …" It was too challenging a question.

"Yes, that was a pretty good seizure you had this morning." Some people are always so positive. "They must've got lots of useful information from it."

"Uh-huh."

She reached for the clipboard hanging at the end of my bed and studied the contents.

"Had a bowel motion today?" This was just standard how's-the-weather kind of talk for her.

"Can't remember. What day is it?"

She laughed. "It's Wednesday, Anna. I'll just write, *unable to recall*, shall I? I'm sure they'll understand." As she took my blood pressure, she told me, "If the doctors get all the information they need from the fit you had this morning, they might send you home in the next few days."

"Yess!"

While a patient was connected to monitoring equipment, showers were not permitted. You got a bowl and a towel every day, but it wasn't the same as soaking yourself under warm water. My hair was getting oily and my scalp was getting itchy.

"The tea and bickies will be here soon."

"Beautiful. Thank you."

"Anything else you need?"

"No thanks." Normality and seeing Finn, those were the things I needed.

A young, timid guy named Dominic was in the room across the hall. He'd been coming in to say hello every day. Dark-haired and skinny, he, like me, was being tested to assess his condition. They needed to see whether he could have an operation that would separate the two sides of his brain. He had a lot more to worry about than I did.

He wasn't epileptic. He had explained what he was being tested for, but I hadn't really understood it, until I saw how it manifested. His condition reminded me of Dr Jekyll and Mr Hyde. One minute he would be as calm as anybody else. Then, all of a sudden, he would become enraged to the point of being dangerous. Or so it appeared. The difference was extraordinary.

Just after the bright, positive nurse left I noticed him standing in the doorway of his room looking worried, agitated, going from one foot to the other. Perhaps he knew what was about to happen to him.

I moved my hand to the emergency button in case he changed into the other person. The nurses would soon figure out who needed the help. He certainly wouldn't be in any condition to ask for it if he turned into Mr. Hyde. He started yelling. I pressed the buzzer.

The nurses were there in a flash. The alarm sounded. I sat watching as he ranted, screaming as though possessed. The code-grey light on the wall in the corridor flashed. He didn't seem to be aware of anything, even the rage that consumed him. A doctor and three bull-necked security guards came rushing around the corner to subdue him. Gaunt and weak, he had acquired the strength of ten men. The guards were solid as rugby players, but it took all three of them to sit on him so the doctor could then inject him with something. He passed out almost immediately.

It was a hive of activity in the neurology ward – nurses with clipboards, visitors with flowers, security guards sitting on people, doctors with stethoscopes, ringing telephones, possessed patients in need of sedation, laundry staff collecting linen, epileptics having induced seizures, medical staff running to save them from themselves … and here was the tea and bickies lady.

"You wanna cuppa, luv?"

*N*ext day, they told me I could go home.

Dominic was back to his normal self after a good night's sleep, no doubt aided by exhaustion from the effects of the previous day. His condition was severe enough to warrant wearing a helmet all the time.

"Hi. Looks like a nice day out there, doesn't it?" he said as he walked in.

"I guess so, forgot to look. You get so used to being in this place after a few days," I said.

"Oh, I haven't. I don't like it in here, I wish they'd send me home," he said. "I brought you something." He handed me a red rose. Was this to make up for becoming Mr Hyde? A response was required. I wished the earth would swallow me up.

"Thank you. That's lovely," I ventured. "I'll ask for a vase next time a nurse comes in." I placed it on the tray in front of me and invited him to sit in the chair.

He left after a few minutes. I wondered about the kind of life he had.

Epilepsy, I thought to myself. *Big deal.*

*B*ut it was a big deal. Mum, Dad and Finn all seemed to think so. Sitting in her spot at the kitchen table, Mum cringed as she listened to me describe my time in hospital. I was telling them about the MRI machine.

"They give you a buzzer to press if you start getting claustrophobic in there. There's no room to move. It's tubular, like a birth canal I suppose. Then, when it's all finished, they take you back to your room and put a sign on your bed saying 'this person's been injected with a radioactive substance, don't go near them for 24 hours.'"

"Ooh my Gott ..." she said in her characteristic way.

"Yeah, that was a shock to me too."

"So how many times did they give you that stuff, Anna?" Dad sounded protective.

"Twice."

"Two times too many," said Mum.

"They had to or they wouldn't be able to operate on me. They still might not."

"Why is that?" asked Dad.

"They have to make sure they're not operating somewhere close to vital areas of the brain. Like the part that controls your speech."

"Ohhhhh ..." Mum put her head in her hands in despair.

I decided not to tell them about the fellow who went into fits of rage. That could wait for another day.

Dr Jenkins had a folder with my name on it on his desk. The verdict was in.

"We have the results of the tests we did on you at the Austin Hospital, and the news is good. It appears there is a reasonable chance of getting close enough to most of the scar tissue around the site of the wound," he said confidently as he opened the manila folder. There were scans of what I presumed to be my brain from different angles, colors highlighting some areas. For once, words failed me.

"Wow," I said inanely.

He noticed the lack of effort on my part to speak. A small smile passed over his face. He also realised how rare this was.

"So we need to book you in for ..." He proceeded to tell me all the things that had to be done prior to surgery. There were memory and psychological evaluations, as well as emotional assessment and preparation. I must not have been listening quite as intently as I should have been.

"... and you'll need to make a will ..."

"*What?*" He had my full attention again. "I thought you said this was a safe operation."

"With surgery, there's always some risk involved. So it's standard procedure to recommend that this be done," he explained.

"Oh right. It's not because it's *brain* surgery?"

"No." He seemed unperturbed as usual. I could only assume his confidence was warranted. I trusted him, and I wasn't turning back now.

My life had been disrupted, Finn's as well. Not the least of which was being unable to drive in the country. Finn was starting to have more of a social life and needed a chauffeur. How could I deny him that? I didn't mind the idea of having a social life again either. I needed my brain and my licence back.

Temporal Lobe Lesionectomy

"Seeya, Mum. I'll call you every day."

"I *love* you." I gave him one more hug before I got on the train.

"Yeah, yeah. Okay, Mum!" He was almost a teenager. Hugs from Mum in public were soon to be taboo.

Carol had moved to Castlemaine from Maldon the year before. She had offered to look after Finn at her place and get him to school every day while I was gone.

"See you when you get back," she said as she hugged me. "I'll check your letters and feed Sheba. We'll visit her and make sure she's not too lonely." There was no point in taking Sheba to her place. She would just do what cats do and try to find her way back to 58 Green Street.

"Thanks. Les will look in on her too." Les Barkley was one of those salt-of-the-earth people. He and his wife had lived across the street from our house for thirty years. The cross on their front door was apparently not just for decoration. He'd never said a word about his faith until I told him I was going to have brain surgery.

The train was about to depart; the conductor was standing on the platform waiting for me to say my goodbyes. I quickly threw my arms around Emma.

"You'll be absolutely fine," she said with confidence in her voice. I nodded sheepishly to the conductor as I finally boarded the train.

We had everything organised. Carol would take Finn for the week. Emma would be on call if needed. There would be lots of people helping, calling, even praying. The train pulled out. Next time we saw each other I would have half my hair shaved off. I would have to think about a hairstyle to suit the change.

As long as the scalpel doesn't slip and make me a zombie ...

I closed my eyes, chastising myself for the pessimistic thought.

They had shown me to the ward and got me settled. After filling in forms and having some coffee I decided to call Mum and Dad.

"Train trip alright?"

"Yes, Dad. Long trip though. Once you get to Spencer Street station it's still a long way out here." The Austin Hospital was well and truly on the other side of the city. "I haven't really got anything to say. Just wanted to call and say g'day to someone." I was biting my lip to stop myself crying, but I didn't tell him that.

"Fair enough, love. You want to talk to your Mum too?"

"Hello, darling, we'll be thinking of you tomorrow, praying everything goes well," she said.

"Thank you, Mum. Please do pray." The sound in her voice was like a soft warm blanket around me on a cold night. Why couldn't she be that sweet all of the time? I did love her. I told her so.

The phone was at the quieter end of the reception desk. As I hung up I noticed a stack of manila folders. The top file had something stamped on it diagonally in bold capital letters: 'Deceased'.

"Put the bloody thing somewhere else," I mumbled as I went back to the ward. It was almost time for dinner.

Back in the ward, a woman in the bed across from me was intent on one thing: "He's coming to get me. He's coming to get me."

She didn't sound like she meant someone coming to drive her home. Unable to sit up, she was expecting the worst. In amongst groans of discomfort, she would repeat the mantra. "They'll be coming to get me soon, won't be long."

People don't say things like that for no reason. I thought about the 'Deceased' stamp. The reception staff would need it again before long. Me, I wasn't going anywhere. I'd bought a will kit as I'd been instructed to. But you have to fill them out for them to mean something.

"They're coming really soon. It won't be long now."

Better you than me, I thought, very ungraciously.

Twice during the night she woke up saying "Won't be long now, won't be long now."

*F*inally, the day had arrived.

"Thanks, luv. You're right, it's gonna be easy," I told Finn. "You give me a call tonight if you want, or any time at all. I don't know how I'll be tonight after the anesthetic, but give us a call anyway, okay? If I'm too groggy, they'll tell you, and you call back again tomorrow, alright?"

Finn told me he would.

"Good. Talk to you soon. Love you." I hung up the phone. The sooner this was over the better.

There was a man in a yellow jumper coming along the corridor. *I don't usually like it, but that's a nice yellow ...* I thought to myself. The man walked into the ward and headed towards me. It was Dr Jenkins.

"The big day has arrived," he said optimistically.

"Sure has. Nice jumper."

"Thank you. I just came to see how you are before they take you off to surgery; won't be long now."

Did he have to say it that way? My stomach jumped at the thought of the woman in the bed opposite. She was asleep. 'They' had not come and taken her away yet.

"Yes, true, they'll be coming to get me. Won't be long now, won't be long ..." I said dryly.

He cottoned on straight away. Perhaps she was another of his patients. "You'll be fine. You're in good hands," he said encouragingly. "Dr Sarrantini has been doing this for a long time now. He could do it in his sleep."

"I'd rather he stayed awake, thanks. Like I'm gonna be. It's only fair."

"I'll make sure and tell him of your preference," he said with a grin. "You'll be asleep at first," he reminded me. "They'll anaesthetise you so they can do the first part of the operation."

They would put me under, then open my skull to get at my brain. Once they had done this, I would need to be awake. The brain does not feel pain, so it wasn't as gruesome as it sounded. I had told myself this many times, as had everyone else. I suspected it was one of those you-just-had-to-be-there experiences.

"Now, I've got a few more people to call in on this morning," Dr Jenkins said.

"Thanks for dropping in. I wasn't expecting it."

"A service I provide all my patients when they're about to have brain surgery," he said.

"Nice of you."

As the yellow jumper disappeared down the corridor, a nurse came in.

"Morning! Good sleep? You're first cab off the rank today," she said. "The anesthetist will be here shortly. We'll get you all set up and take you to theatre."

"Great. Let's get it over with."

It wasn't great. It was petrifying. I was scared shitless. But these nurses managed to somehow make you believe brain surgery was the best thing that was ever going to happen to you. And perhaps it was. I struggled to subdue the emotions rising inside me as the time drew nearer. *How calm these people are,* I thought. It was as though they were working at a supermarket check-out – nothing out of the ordinary, just another day. Like airline pilots, you have to be a certain kind of person. More nurses had arrived and were bustling around my bed, getting me ready to be wheeled out.

Funny the things you think about when you're trying to block out what's going on around you. I couldn't afford to recognise how scared I was. So now, instead of focusing on how self-disciplined the nurses were, I used concern for hair as a distraction.

They injected the anaesthetic. I reminded them, "Don't cut too much hair off … Only as much a … …"

I regained consciousness surrounded by people in surgical gowns.

"Ah, just in time," said someone. It sounded as though everything was going according to plan.

"G'day," I said, as heartily as possible.

"G'day," said someone else.

"Now, we've made an opening in your skull and we're going to probe around your brain to get an idea of where we can go and where we can't," the surgeon told me. I knew he was the surgeon. He sounded like he knew he was in charge. You become tuned in to what's going on around you when you're strapped to a bed with your head in a cage to stop it from moving.

"Now, Anna, you've been told what the procedure is, but I'll go through it with you again, just to make sure we all understand each other, alright?"

"Yep." He wouldn't get any resistance from me.

"I will find an area in your left temporal lobe and I will say something. Then I will ask you to repeat what I have said. If you can, we know it's safe to operate near that area of the brain. If you are not able to repeat it, we know to proceed with caution in that area. This will enable us to operate on you within the safest parameters possible. Make sense?"

"Yes, it makes sense," I replied. "Hope it still does tomorrow. Sorry, sorry, I shouldn't have said that!"

I could hear one of them laugh softly.

"It's okay. We know you weren't being critical of our surgeon. This isn't something that happens to a person every day," he said kindly.

I was trying not to laugh now. I had to get my nerves under control.

"So, can you take a deep breath in?" asked another nurse. "And let it out slowly. That's it." There was affection in her voice.

"Thanks. I'm good now," I said.

"We'll make a start, then. Here's the first thing I want you to repeat," said the surgeon. He waited a few seconds before he said, "There is a ship on the horizon." His voice was soothing. He sounded in control.

"There is a ship on the horizon," I repeated.

"Europe is a continent."

"Europe is a continent." That reminded me of Mum, which reminded me of Dad, which reminded me of Finn. Were they thinking of me right then?

"There are seven days in a week."

"There are seven days in a week," I repeated.

This went on for a few more sentences; then he said, "The library is open."

This must have been an area of my brain not to mess with. I had heard him say, "The library is open." My intent was to repeat it, as I'd been instructed. But the words would not come out.

"I'm going to say that again, Anna. The library is open. Can you repeat that back to me?"

I couldn't. It was extraordinary. I heard him make an aside to one of the nurses. They acknowledged it, making a note of what had just transpired.

"Were you unable to repeat what I said just a moment ago? The library is open?"

"That's right doctor. I couldn't say it," I told him.

"Alright. So, we'll keep going then, shall we? I'll say something and you repeat it."

"Okay," I answered.

"One plus one equals two," he said.

"One plus one equals two," I replied, relieved I could.

"The rain in Spain falls mainly on the plain."

There it was again. Nothing was coming out. Literally speechless, I burst into tears. A nurse was beside me straight away assuring me all was well.

"It's alright, Anna."

"I know it is. It's just what you said might happen."

"That's right. It's all part of the operation and it will benefit you in the long-run."

"Yes, yes. Thank you."

"You're doing extremely well. You okay to go on now?"

"Yes, I am."

It only happened once more. After that, it was time for them to remove the scar tissue that had been making life so hard. It took more than an hour. I lay on the operating table thinking calm thoughts, waiting for it to be over. If these competent, composed people reminded me of airline pilots, then having brain surgery was like air travel. You know you have to board the plane if you want to reach your destination. You also know you're going to feel a whole lot better once you've landed.

They'd taken as much scar tissue away as they could. All that was left to do was put the piece of skull they'd removed back in place.

"Now we just have to do a bit more drilling," announced the surgeon calmly. I'd been anaesthetised when they drilled into my head the first time. Was it that word 'drilling' that put me on the defensive? Or was it the actual sound? It was just like one of the drills Dad kept in his shed. This was more than I could bear. Survival instinct kicked in.

"Stop, NOW!" I ordered them. It was as if Finn had just run out on the road in front of a car. Nothing else mattered. They were drilling into my skull. It was like a movie I would never watch.

In his cultured, calm voice, Doctor Sarrantini said, "I suppose we'll have to then." It was a classic. If I hadn't been in fight or flight mode I would have laughed. Somebody must have turned a dial somewhere to supply me with more of whatever chemicals they use to keep people happy and chilled-out on the operating table.

Next thing I knew, I was being wheeled out of theatre attached to drips, someone pushing the bed, someone else navigating, another person making sure the drip was being wheeled at the same speed. The surgeon was holding the rail on the bed, talking to one of the others. I grabbed his hand and kissed it as though he were the Pope or the Dalai Lama. It was over the top. I didn't care.

"Thank you. *Thank you.*"

"That's perfectly alright, Anna. All part of a day's work," he replied.

In Intensive Care, the nurse came checking on me regularly, taking pulse, blood pressure, temperature, shining a torch into my eyes.

"Feel like something to eat?" she asked.

"Mm, yes please," I said eagerly.

After dinner, she came in again and asked how I was.

"Good th...aaaauuuuuugh," I replied in a somewhat undignified manner. Dinner had been nice, but my stomach did not agree. The nurse was not impressed. The expression on her face said, *Yeah, right, chuck your guts on My shift, why don'tcha?*

Next day, they took me back to the ward I'd been in before the operation. The woman who believed 'they' were coming to get her had been correct. She was gone. In her place was a woman who'd had a stomach operation. Another new admission was a girl with a mental deficiency.

"No, No! I want, I want, I want ..."

She had been in a bicycle accident. I wasn't sure if this had made her mentally disabled or if the disability had caused the accident. Either way, she was providing the nurses with plenty of work.

"I'm so hungry," I said to the nurse. Then I remembered throwing up the night before.

At that moment an unwanted memory from my party-hard past came back to haunt me. Almost twenty years before, I had said exactly the same thing to some people whose couch I'd slept on after a night on the scotch. The two virtual strangers had rolled their eyes at that point, no doubt hoping *persona non grata* would depart as soon as possible. In an instant I had realised why I was so hungry, and also how very unwelcome I had made myself. Needless to say they had not offered to make me breakfast, and I had left in disgrace.

Now, here I was in hospital after brain surgery. Decades ago, in that party-hard past, I had been in a car with someone twice as drunk as I was. He had driven us off the road. When the second car accident happened, I'd hit my head in the same place. But if the first accident hadn't happened, the second would not have given me epilepsy. It served me right. *It's karma. As you sow, so shall you reap*, I thought to myself.

Temporary respite from regret and pain came in the form of morphine. So, not only did I have real visitors, like Mum and Dad, there were imaginary, hallucinogenic ones as well.

The first apparition to appear before me was a British-looking man wearing a three-piece suit, bow tie, bowler hat, handkerchief sticking out of the pocket of his suit coat. He was carrying a briefcase, old fashioned of course. He certainly wouldn't have had a mobile but would definitely have had a fob watch. He seemed to be just standing there. Perhaps waiting for a double-decker bus? It did not arrive.

Then there was a little girl dancing at the foot of my bed. She was wearing a sweet mauve dress with lace frills. She had a magic wand in her hand, fairy wings and beautiful, curly hair cascading down her back.

Later, there was a man wearing full Middle Eastern regalia – fez hat, baggy trousers, long dress-like top and sandals. The most intricate embroidery adorned the cuffs of his trousers and sleeves.

There were cats and dogs as well, some playing around with each other, some with the girl in fairy clothes. But the most surreal was the jumper. It was made from some kind of home-spun wool, dark brown, angora perhaps. It walked past the bed and right out the window. We were several storeys high. But it didn't matter; there was nobody in it.

The scenery was starting to change from built-up, semi-rural to wide-open spaces. Next thing, our town's name was at the top of the green and white sign. It was over. Paramedics were driving me home from the most remarkable experience of my life.

"Anna! So glad to see you home, luv." It was Les from across the road, running over with his arms open wide to greet me. He hugged me like he hadn't seen me in years. He must have meant it when he said he would pray.

"I'm so glad to be back." I hugged him with gratitude.

The ambulance attendant carried my things onto the porch, said goodbye and left. After Les helped me in with my bags and made us a cup of tea, he left as well. The lounge room had a skylight. I stood under it and looked over at the compact kitchen, the purple couch, the wall plastered with cheap posters. This was my life. I saw my reflection in the mirror, half my hair missing, like a teenage girl trying to shock her parents. My head hurt.

I wasn't a teenage girl anymore, and yet I was still paying for the mistakes I'd made when I had been one. That first car accident had caused a chain of events that would haunt me until the day I died.

Thank God for this place, this sanctuary.

At least this was something I could say I'd gotten right, this home of ours. Here it was possible to sit, be calm and think. Relief overcame me. I was safe. I took two of the pain killers they had loaded me up with and went to bed.

Status

One morning, five months later, Finn knocked on my bedroom door looking deeply troubled.

"Mum. You better come and have a look at this."

"What's the matter?" Was Sheba sick?

"Just come and look." He was quite serious, as if someone had killed themselves. Indeed someone had, several in fact. There, on the television screen, were scenes of the 9/11 terrorist attacks that changed our world forever.

We sat on the couch together and watched as they played the same footage over and over again. The twin World Trade Centre buildings glistened as the sun reflected off the windows. The first plane flew towards them, eventually bringing the building down like a deck of cards. Minutes later, another plane slammed into the second tower.

I thought of all the action movies I had seen since Finn had started watching TV. Had we been numbed by them? Wasn't it a bit too easy to sit there and feel nothing while watching it?

I put my arm around him and kissed the top of his head. Did I realise how lucky we both were? We had a house to come home to, life in a country where soldiers did not parade down the street with rifles over their shoulders. Where you could be fairly certain that when you walked out the door, your life would not be in danger. Where children, like the one I had my arm around, could go to school and get an education instead of a bomb. Where the country you lived in, and the house you dwelt in, could be called 'home'.

A month later, I was the one knocking on Finn's door. I'd woken up aching all over, and I had bitten my tongue. The doctors had begun reducing the medicine I took, believing I didn't need as much since I hadn't had a fit for six months after the surgery.

"Finn." I opened the door. It was a Saturday morning. He was still asleep.

"What, Mum? It's too early!"

"Yeah, yeah, I know it is, sorry. I had a fit in my sleep." I sat on the edge of the bed. His crankiness turned to concern.

"No way, Mum. You okay?"

"I suppose. A hug will help." He obliged.

I called Carol, and she drove us both to hospital where they put me in a waiting room.

"I'll take Finn to my place. I'll be home all day," she told me, "so when they're ready to send you home, they can give me a call. I'll give them my number on the way out."

"Thank you for driving me here. I don't know how long this will take." I hugged them both. "Carol will look after you, Finn."

"You'll be okay, Mum."

Next thing I knew, I was in a hospital bed. I didn't remember anything about that morning or any time ever. I knew my mind had gone empty, but had no idea what had ever been in it. Except that my name was Anna McAllister, that I had a son and that his name was Finn McAllister.

Who are you? Who am I? I knew the answers. He would have been proud of me. I would have visualised him sitting with me on the couch waiting for me to answer him. Except for the fact that I had no recollection of all the times he had done so. I hardly even knew what he looked like. In my mind's eye was a picture of a house; our house? That was all there was. Except for a vague sense that there was much, much more and that I had no access to any of it.

"You're awake. That was a good sleep," said a nurse who had just come in.

"Huh?"

"You've been asleep all day. You needed a rest, that's for sure."

"Why?" I asked.

"You went into *status epilepticus*," she replied.

"Sorry?" Was that a fancy way of saying I'd had a fit?

"*Status epilepticus*," she repeated. "It's when you have one fit after another," she said, as if I ought to have known.

"What the fuck?" A slight frown passed across the nurse's face. "Sorry."

"It's okay. You've had a big day."

"You can have more than one fit at a time?"

"Oh yes, it's a very serious condition. You can die from it," she said matter-of-factly.

"*Die* from epilepsy? You can't die from epilepsy."

"Well you can actually," she said reassuringly. "It doesn't happen very often. We stabilised you, so there's nothing to worry about now. We're going to keep you here for a few more days, just to make sure you're a hundred per cent before we send you home."

"Right. What happened? How many fits did I have? How many hours have I been sleeping? What time is it? What *day* is it?"

The nurse tried to slow me down. "One thing at a time, Anna."

"What happened?" I replied

"You were in there," she gestured in the direction of the room they'd put me in when I arrived. "Someone heard a noise and went to check on you. They found you convulsing and banging your head on the floor." Was this the true definition of 'head-banger'?

"Then what?" I asked incredulously.

"We moved you onto a mattress and gave you an injection to stop the seizure. But you started fitting again, so we gave you something else. You had three more seizures before you started responding to the injections. Then we moved you here once we'd got them under control."

"And what did you call it?"

"*Status epilepticus.*"

"*Status epilepticus*. And how long have I been asleep?

"All day."

It was just what I wanted to keep doing.

After two days in hospital, my doctor came to see me before they discharged me. He'd spoken to Dr Jenkins. They both seemed to think it was a one-off. He was explaining why they thought this.

"Although it was a s*tatus epilepticus* attack, your neurologist and I have spoken over the phone, and we're pretty sure the reason it happened has something to do with reduction of Dilantin levels in your bloodstream."

"It was the worst seizure I've ever had. I let people probe around in my brain because I thought it was going to make things better. There's no way I would have gone through all that if I thought it was going to make it worse." He was going to have to say something convincing before I felt assured. In the meantime, I sat staring vacantly, waiting to hear something I understood, something that would give me reason to be optimistic again.

"Epilepsy is a very complex condition," he said.

"That's becoming more and more apparent," I said dryly.

"We reduced your dose too quickly. Your brain reacted by making you have a fit. Now you're back on the dose you were on before we started reducing it. We'll keep you on that for a month. After that, as long as you don't have any more seizures, we'll reduce it by *half* as much as we did before. If you're alright with that, it will probably mean your *status epilepticus* event was the result of coming off too quickly."

"I see. Is it a common thing?" That would help, to know if the same thing happened to other people.

"Yes, it's fairly common. What I'm saying is, it's the most likely scenario, especially considering you haven't had any trouble since the surgery." That sounded encouraging.

"Thank God for that," I said.

"Well, we'll just have to see how things go." How many times had I heard that?

I had to ask. "Is it possible the surgery has made things worse?"

"No." He sounded quite definite. "I doubt that very much, Anna. Don't concern yourself as far as that goes."

The walk home was pleasant. My fears had been alleviated. Now it was just a matter of waiting. Although it was comforting to hear the doctor explain what had probably happened, the threat of a fit was a constant boogieman following me everywhere I went. Even after major surgery, it seemed it always would be.

Once I got home, the couch was comfortable, but the bed was better. The doona was like a reassuring embrace. It occurred to me that it wouldn't hurt to pray or meditate. I fell asleep instead.

Another month later, having dinner at Carol's, we watched with dismay as the election count on television showed that we would retain our Liberal government.

"That's the thing about democracy. You have to put up with the Liberals as well," I said dejectedly, slumping in the armchair.

"Yes, true, but then things could be so much worse. He hasn't dismantled Medicare. Yet."

"Yeah. How would people with no money pay for things like, say, a temporal lobe lesionectomy, without medical benefits?"

We tried to find something good to say about John Howard, the prime minister who had just been re-elected.

"He did recall all those guns," she said. "That was a good move."

"It certainly was. And he walks every morning," I said. "And he and his wife walk everywhere holding hands. I think that's sweet."

"It is." We weren't completely heartless.

Buddha, Dharma, Sangha

It was now only a matter of days before I could drive again. My licence had been suspended for a year after surgery.

Because of the surgery, I was sometimes the recipient of compassion and, at times, its unhealthy cousin, pity. I was in the supermarket when an older woman walking past me couldn't help but notice my hair. The side I'd been operated on had only grown back a few inches. I had no intention of cutting the rest to match, so it must have looked like a statement of rebelliousness. I was about to turn forty, so rebelliousness had long since subsided, replaced by a more cautious, circumspect approach to life.

"Looks a bit odd, doesn't it?" I said to her.

The woman seemed embarrassed at having been caught looking. "Sorry," she said.

"No, it's fine. I had brain surgery, you see. They had to shave this area," I told her, pointing. "Hair styling isn't included in post-operative care. It should be, shouldn't it?"

"Ha! That's a good idea. What did you have brain surgery for?"

"Epilepsy," I told her. "And I get the feeling it's worked. They haven't let me drive for a year, but the year is up on Friday," I told her excitedly.

"Congratulations," she said. We went our different ways. My hairstyle was like a dog – I was having conversations with total strangers about it.

A bit further along, I saw Alisha who was in one of the singing groups I'd been involved in since living in Castlemaine. She belonged to the growing section of our community that had moved up from Melbourne to live a wholesome, politically correct, organic, new-age lifestyle. She exuded an aura of sublime peace and tranquility, literally all the time. I wasn't buying it for a minute.

"*Anna*," she said earnestly, her head tilted, a smile of sadness and commiseration on her face. "How *are* you?"

"I'm doing really well," I told her. But she continued to look at me with abject pity on her face, waiting for me to break down and tell her I was actually on the verge of suicide. "At least I was till you came up looking at me as if I'd lost everything that matters."

Her demeanor changed instantly. Pity was replaced by indignation.

"Yeah, well, sorry 'bout that. But sometimes you've just got to say something, even if it isn't gonna go down very well."

Was that ungracious? I wondered to myself as I walked away. *She'll survive it*, I decided.

The year was up. The surgery had been a success. The *status epilepticus* event had been a one-off, as the doctors had suspected. Finally, I could get behind the wheel again.

Finn had thick semi-curly hair and was growing it long. He was now a teenager, which I thought had something to do with it. He had washed it that morning and waited until I put my seat belt on, then shook his head, like a dog coming out of a dam.

"You did that on purpose," I said as I started the Kingswood.

"Duuh, Mum, of course I did," he said with a cheeky grin.

After driving him to school, I headed out of town and drove to Bendigo for no other reason than because I could. The train ran parallel to the highway on the way to Harcourt. The stereo was on.

It was a balmy morning in central Victoria. In a couple of weeks, I would be taking Lyn to Geelong. In my car. We were going to hear the Dalai Lama speak.

As we drove along the freeway, we were talking about the schedule His Holiness kept.

"I'm glad I don't have to travel as much as he does," said Lyn.

"Yes, flying everywhere," I said, remembering my one experience of being in the air. "When I came back from New Zealand there was *turbulence*," I told her, using the American accent of the captain who had informed us of what was going on. "Not in any hurry to experience that again."

"I've been on planes that have flown in those sorts of conditions, nothing too dramatic, thankfully."

"They say flying is actually the safest form of travel."

"I'm sure it didn't feel that way to you at the time," Lyn said understandingly.

I started wondering about the safety of flying as compared with driving. But I decided not to go there, either in my head or in conversation with Lyn, my passenger. *She accepted my offer of a lift,* I reminded myself silently.

"Apparently it was nothing, compared to what can happen."

"Yes, it's a different world up there."

"Thank you for driving us, Anna. I've been looking forward to this."

"My pleasure. So glad I can drive again. In Melbourne you can get away without having a car. When I moved to Castlemaine, I had no idea I'd end up epileptic," I said.

"Would you have stayed in Melbourne if you did?"

"I would still have come. But I would have put a lot more thought into what I would do if I wasn't allowed to drive."

"Isn't it a good thing we don't know what's going to happen to us in the future? Some of us would be too scared to walk out our front doors," she said, laughing.

"I'm glad I didn't know I was going to be on an operating table making conversation with them while they operated on my brain."

"I don't know how you went through with it."

"I had to. Got sick of being on the edge of my seat all the time, wondering what was going to happen next."

"Finn must be glad you can drive again."

"Oh yes. They're all starting to want to hang out with their mates now instead of being at home with their parents, so they need chauffeurs."

"It's the age when it starts happening." Lyn had five children, so she knew this well.

"That's right. It's what they're supposed to be doing at this age. I don't want to be overprotective with him. I notice changes in him, and I start wondering what it's going to be like when he leaves home. In these past couple of years, it's like we aren't '1' and '1a' anymore. We're '1' and '2', you know what I mean?"

"It's called breaking away from one another."

The city skyline always had a blanket of smog over it, on either the top or the bottom half, occasionally both. Today it was over the top. Geelong was another two hours away.

The venue for the Dalai Lama's talk was the Geelong football oval. In the centre of the oval was a large marquee with an elevated chair in the middle. Monks dressed in yellow and red surrounded it. They had prayer beads and were chanting a mantra. It was scheduled to start shortly. I wondered where he would make his entrance from.

"I wonder if they'll have one of those big pieces of cloth for him to run through like the footy teams do," I said to someone next to me. They liked the idea, but doubted it very much. "No, I don't think so either. But where's he going to come from?"

One of the monks put his prayer beads around his neck and got up. Something was happening. It was about to start. He moved to the centre, climbed the steps leading to the chair and sat down.

It was His Holiness. He'd been there the whole time.

"And at the end of the talk he had one more thing to say, 'Smile at people. But make sure it's genuine.'"

Carol laughed. "We must seem serious compared to other people around the world," she said.

"We must."

"Where did you get the exercise bike from?" she asked, pointing to my new toy in the corner of the room.

"A woman from the folk music scene said she was getting rid of it. I just read a book about healthy eating, so I thought it was good timing."

"Good for you. You've been looking a lot better since the surgery. I can imagine the difference it's made."

"It's like being in a small, dark, dusty room with the windows shut," I told her. "Then the blinds get pulled up, the windows get opened and the sun streams in. It's almost worth getting epilepsy just to feel the difference … or maybe not …"

"What's that, Mum?" Finn had come into the kitchen and seen the concoction I was making.

"It's a thick shake from this recipe book," I told him, as I turned on the blender. Curious but doubtful, he looked at the mixture.

"It's got sunflower seeds, almonds, soy milk, lecithin and blueberries."

"Can I have a taste?"

"Sure." I poured it into a large glass. He took a sip and cringed. "It's good for you," I said encouragingly.

"Good on you, Mum," he said as he opened the fridge. "So is milk."

There were no soft drinks in our house. Our budget was tight, but our food was good. Finn would go through major changes in the next few years, and calcium was one of the many things he would need. He would need me less, and more at the same time. I was glad the epilepsy seemed to be under control, the drama over. Other dramas were sure to arise as my son became an adolescent.

Part Two

The times they are a-changin'

Finn was getting zits and teenage attitude. The growth spurt was starting. I was looking forward to being forty for some reason I couldn't understand. Invites had gone out for the party which would last all weekend. (I would regret that decision because it would later be something Finn would expect for his eighteenth.)

Elaine's husband had died a long time before we got there. She'd lived across the road for decades, next to Les and Rose Barkley, Les was the man who said he would pray for me when I had brain surgery. Now she lived on her own with her dog and cat. A gentleman came and drove her to church every Sunday morning. She was the epitome of the conservative Christian element of their generation – no smoking, drinking, carousing – no bad behaviour of any kind. Considering this, the open mindedness of this Baptist lady astounded me on the Saturday afternoon of the party.

People who couldn't make it were coming over with presents and birthday wishes. Elaine came over with a plate of scones, telling me she would not be staying for the party. I hadn't really expected she would, but she had been so nice to us over the years I had invited her anyway.

"Many happy returns, Anna," she said in her gentle voice.

"Will you stay for a cuppa? We can have a scone."

"That would be very nice," she said.

I put the kettle on and got the butter. There was another knock at the door. Simon, someone I knew from the folk music scene in our town, had come to give me a block of hash. In something of a quandary I accepted the gift.

"It's just that … I don't smoke this stuff anymore, not for a long time," I told him. It wasn't just because of the elderly white-haired Christian woman sitting at the table. He had never seen me smoke grass. I was sure of that because I had stopped smoking it a long time before Finn was even a twinkle in John's eye, as the saying went. John, even though he was a hippy back then, had never been that big on it either.

Simon waved his hand in the air, and said "It's okay. You do what you like with it. That's your birthday gift from me." I reluctantly took the gift and introduced the two of them. "Simon, this is Elaine. Elaine, this is Simon."

Simon had been smoking weed for a large chunk of his life the way other people smoke cigarettes. He was on another planet virtually all the time. Occasionally he believed himself to be God. Thankfully, on the afternoon in question, he did not. I gave a subtle nod to the Buddha on our mantelpiece in gratitude for this. He did, however, proceed to roll a joint then and there. As I watched, flabbergasted, I imagined Elaine felt that it had been the right decision to bring the scones over and go home again. I was glad Finn was at a friend's house for the night, or he would have been passively smoking it. So would Elaine very shortly, for that matter. But neither of them seemed the slightest bit uncomfortable, so I supposed I oughtn't to be either. I made them both a cup of tea. Elaine and I ate buttered scones while Simon smoked his joint.

The party had been a raging success. Bonfire in the backyard, lots of people, singing, music, food and laughter. Uncle Jim had played the spoons to accompany the fiddles and guitars.

"I'm going to have to speak to Elaine about the other day," I told Finn as I drove him to school.

"Why? What happened?"

"That's right, you weren't there, were you? Good thing too. Simon came around a few hours before the party and gave me a present."

"What's wrong with that?"

"It was hashish, marijuana in other words."

"I *know* what it is, Mum."

"I presume you don't know *too* much about it?"

"No, Mum, of course not," he said.

"Good. And that's the way it's going to stay if I have anything to do with it."

"Don't worry, Mum. You worry too much."

"It's only because I care."

From the corner of my eye I saw his face soften momentarily, but only for a moment. He was getting too old for all that motherly-love shit.

"They told us all about drugs at school, Mum," he said. I kept my eyes on the road even though I wanted to look over at him and say, *What?* I had been under the impression I was the one who was meant to talk to him about those things. We had a green arrow. I didn't pursue the topic.

"Anyway, the point is, when Simon came around, Elaine was there. She'd brought a plate of scones. While I boiled the kettle, he rolled a joint." Finn went into hysterics thinking about of the two of them in the same room.

"It was pretty funny I guess," I admitted.

"Did she have any?"

"*No*, Finn. She certainly did *not*. And neither did I."

Later, I sat at her kitchen table while she put the hand-knitted tea-cosy on the teapot.

"Look, Elaine, I just wanted to come over and say how sorry I am about the other day. When you were there and that friend of mine came over? When he started rolling that cigarette? I don't know if you know what it was he was …"

"Oh yes, I know what it was!" A look of wry amusement came over her face.

"I can't believe he started smoking it right there in front of you. I'm so embarrassed."

"It's alright. You weren't to know." She placed a cup and saucer in front of me and got out the biscuit tin.

"You didn't get stoned, did you?" I couldn't resist asking.

"No, Anna, I didn't," she answered matter-of-factly.

"Well, that's good. Neither did I."

"I'm glad to hear it," she answered with a very slight smile. We waited for the tea to draw.

"And by the way, Elaine, please don't get the impression that people come around and light up joints in my house as a matter of course, will you? That really, truly, was not something I expected to happen."

I could do with more people like her in my life; people who made tea in pots and put tea-cosies on them. Fewer people who thought it was perfectly okay to smoke marijuana in front of elderly women, not to mention in front of my son, had he been there.

One night a few weeks later, Finn and I were on the couch after dinner. A show on TV was not grabbing our attention.

"There's some stuff I've been meaning to talk to you about," I said with trepidation.

"Why? What's going on?" He sounded concerned. "Did the doctor tell you something?"

"No, luv. Nothing like that. This is just stuff every parent is supposed to talk to their kids about." I got up and turned down the TV. I thought I might as well launch straight into it. "Ahem, … the facts of life. I'm supposed to talk to you about all tha …"

"It's okay, Mum. I know all about it," he said, stifling a laugh.

"Excuse me? You better not know all about it. How could you possibly know about that stuff?" He was too young to know about those things. I was about to discover I was living in the past.

"They taught us in primary school." He really was laughing now. Apparently I'd left this talk much too late for someone of his generation. They'd told him about drugs. They'd told him about sex. I wondered when the teachers were going to come around and do my housework as well. Somehow I had the feeling that day would never come.

"Don't parents get the chance to tell their kids those kinds of things anymore? When did they tell you about it?"

"Grade four," he said matter-of-factly. My dropping jaw and popping eyes made him laugh even more.

"So you know how girls get pregnant?"

"Yes, Mum, of course," he said with mortification in his voice.

"There was no 'of course' about it in my day. So they told you about contraception as well?"

"Yes!" he insisted, eager to change the subject.

"God almighty, this was meant to be a significant conversation …"

"It's okay, Mum. I don't even have a girlfriend."

"Of course you don't have a girlfriend. You're not old enough to start doing things like that … Oh well, that's one thing to cross off my list of things to do. If I can't inform you about one of the most important aspects of life, can I at least make you a cup of tea?"

"Yes, Mum," he said with a grin. "And thanks for saying all that."

"All part of the job description, darling. Well, at least it used to be."

My sheltered upbringing meant I was sixteen before anyone told me anything. What did a modest, clean-living Latvian girl need to know, after all? Lie back and think of Latvia, but only once you got married, and even then, never on Sundays.

So he'd been given The Talk. It was good that schools were recognising the need to get rid of prudish attitudes. Even so, I felt cheated. They'd taken away one of my duties.

As I came back to the couch with our tea, we turned our attention back to the television. Another program was starting.

"Hey! I know this guy!"

"You *know* him?" Finn asked dubiously.

"Not personally, just who he is: Ozzy Osbourne, lead singer of Black Sabbath. At least he used to be."

That caught Finn's attention. The show was called *The Osbourne's*, a reality drama based on this rock star fellow and his family.

"Black Sabbath," I told him, "are known as the fathers of heavy metal. Did you know *that*?" Here was something I could teach him about. "You will have heard their music. I listen to it sometimes. That one I was trying to copy the solo from?"

"I know the one you mean, Mum." He had seen me in front of the cassette player rewinding the guitar solo from *Paranoid*, trying to play it on my acoustic guitar.

"A simple solo, but so effective. When played properly, that is …"

"You're getting better at it, Mum."

"Thanks."

"Hey, why is someone like him wearing a cross?" Finn wanted to know.

"I can tell you exactly why," I said. "They did a gig in the seventies one time. When they got back to their hotel, there was a bunch of Satanists waiting for them in the foyer. They wanted them to join their cult, bless it or something." Finn thought this was hilarious. I proceeded to tell him how they responded. "They reacted by saying 'We don't worship the devil, we play heavy metal music. Bugger off or we'll call security.' The Satanists put a curse on them for that, and they got worried. So they started wearing crosses, especially on stage, so people wouldn't get the wrong idea about their music."

The program followed Ozzy Osbourne and his wife Sharon around their rock star mansion as they went about their daily activities. The gym, pool, ornate kitchen and majestic staircase were a perfect backdrop for their lives and their teenage children, who were pretending to look oh-so-bored.

"He's wearing black nail polish," Finn observed with concern. Ozzy Osbourne was waving his hands around in a theatrical manner as he talked.

"Goes with all the rings on his fingers, don't you think?"

"I suppose so." Finn wasn't convinced.

"Goes with the craziness in his face too," I added.

"No. He's acting for TV," Finn said. Nobody was going to pull the wool over this boy's eyes.

"I'm not so sure about that, Finn," I replied.

"This guy's a try-hard," he said, shaking his head. I loved the expressions he'd been coming out with lately.

I wasn't so sure about the ones Ozzy Osbourne was coming out with though. The show had fifteen minutes to go. I got a pen and paper. Every time Ozzy swore, I marked it down and showed the paper to Finn when the program ended.

"Forty-six times in a quarter of an hour," I said in clipped tones. "I don't think I've ever heard someone swear as much as that in my whole life. Unbelievable." I felt I'd done my parental duty. Not that I didn't use colourful language at times. But there were limits to everything.

It didn't stop us from watching the show every week from then on. For me to watch a show like that as a teenager (even if there had been anything remotely like it) would have been as likely as being told the facts of life in primary school. Times sure had changed.

Generation Gap

In the words of Geoffrey Chaucer, "*Time and tide wait for no man.*" I had turned forty and was officially middle-aged. Finn was also ageing somewhat. A whole fifteen years had gone past since the morning he popped out onto the sea-grass matting in the lounge room.

His eyebrows were thickening, his shoulders broadening, and he was getting his father's hooky nose. There was something else about him that could not be identified in physical features. It hadn't kicked in yet, but it was starting, that look-out-I'm-male-and-I'm-here attitude. It wasn't for his Mum to say how cute he was anymore. But the girls would soon be telling him.

The bookcase had marks on it indicating his height at various ages. But it was becoming 'uncool' to be led by his Mum to see how much he'd grown. This particular evening was a different matter, however. He'd finally done it. I marked his height on the bookcase. It was now a centimetre more than mine. Going to the kitchen to start dinner, I watched as my teenage lad sauntered to his room. He made a detour and moved towards me, putting his face close up to mine.

"Hello, short person," he said.

*H*ad I been allowed to watch it as a teenager, *Countdown* is what I would have grown up with. At least I had been allowed to listen to the radio and buy records. One of the first albums I ever bought was Black Sabbath's *Heaven and Hell*. It had always perplexed me that Mum never said anything about the band name or the title, not to mention the music itself. It was far from Bach or Schubert.

ABC TV had replaced *Countdown* with a show called *Rage,* and, of course, I allowed Finn to watch it. Sometimes we'd watch it together or with his mates who had stayed overnight. But, as adolescence set in, they would retreat into his room and watch it on his TV.

As Finn started heading into adolescence, it was as if there were two separate worlds co-existing under the same roof. The issues and interests I discussed with my friends started to be referred to as 'lame' (foolish) or 'gross' (revolting). More positive expressions like 'sick' (great) or 'awesome' (fantastic) were also to be heard in our house. 'Gay' did not mean homosexual any longer. Needless to say, it didn't mean happy either. It meant something not even worthy of consideration.

An 'emo' wore black clothes and, in an emotional way, dwelt on the angst of life. A 'dweeb' was someone who was overly concerned with the academic side of life. A 'Goth' was someone who wore dark clothes, piercings and long straggly hair, often dyed various colours.

Gareth was a Goth. To watch him and his mates walk down the street was like seeing a moving work of art. It was not to everyone's taste, but I found the long ripped coats, pierced ears, eyebrows, nose and general attitude very refreshing. He didn't give a stuff what anyone thought of him. Or if he did, he was doing an excellent impersonation of someone who did not.

James was Gareth's younger brother and a frequent guest at our house. He, Finn and another mate Craig were in his room enjoying a late breakfast with *Rage* music in the background. Craig was someone I had started to see a lot of in our house. He was tall and would get taller. The purple couch with its four seats would prove invaluable to him when he stayed overnight.

One morning, I was sitting at the computer Finn had been teaching me not to be afraid of. I recognised a tune coming from the next room. It was a cover of *Baker Street*. But this wasn't Gerry Rafferty's laid-back version. It was heavy metal or, to be more precise, grunge. I went into Finn's room to find out who the band was.

"The Foo Fighters, Mum," he told me.

"Never heard of them."

"Wikipedia."

"Never heard of them either."

"Oh my God!" said one of them, unsuccessfully stifling a laugh. Someone as out of touch as me provided teenagers with an endless source of mirth. After the laughter subsided, Finn explained that Wikipedia was not a band but an internet web site that provided you with information on practically anything. He suggested I find out more about it.

"Yeah, okay, when the song's over." I sat down on the bed, moving someone's smelly feet out of the way.

> "He's got this dream about buying some land
> He's gonna give up the crack and the one-night stands
> And then he'll settle down
> In some quiet little town
> and forget about everything ..."

"Crack?"

"It's a drug, Mum."

"Yeah, I know *that*, luv. It's just that the guy who wrote this song in the seventies said 'booze' not 'crack'."

What was alcohol these days? Water? Was it not an issue anymore compared to the other kinds of trouble you could get yourself into?

The internet was still something to be reckoned with. My generation had to become part of the electronic age or we would be left behind. Some of us jumped. Some of us had to be pushed. Finn and his mates seemed to understand the meaning of all the new words and phrases, even why the new devices did what they did. I had found a Wikipedia website about the Foo Fighters, as I'd been encouraged to.

"Look at this willya? Me First and the Gimme-Gimmes!"

"What's that Mum?"

"The name of a band one of the Foo Fighters' guitarists was in. And he was in this one too, No Use for a Name. I'm not so sure about that. I'm much more likely to remember Me First and the Gimme-Gimmes."

He was glad, maybe even a bit relieved, that I was getting the hang of the computer. He sat down at the desk with me.

"Sunny Day Real Estate. Ha!"

We both laughed at the name of another band one of the Foo Fighters had been in.

"Their name is taken from the World War Two term foo-fighter," I read from the computer screen, "used to refer to unidentified flying objects. And look, how about this for an album title, *The Colour and the Shape*."

You could spend hours on these sites if you weren't careful.

Skateboarding had become Finn and his mates' favourite thing to do. One afternoon, I heard him come up the front steps. When I turned to look, I saw he had half a skateboard in one hand, the other half in the other, a look of defeat on his face. My heart sank, and the cash register in my head went 'ka-ching'. Another hundred bucks? Where would I find it this time? This would be the third skateboard I would buy him, not counting the one he bought on eBay that never came.

"Hey, Mum," he said unenthusiastically.

"G'day. What happened?"

"It broke in half," he said cynically.

"Yes, luv, I can see that. How?"

"There's some steps at the south school that are really good to ollie," he told me. "I came down too hard and it snapped." And then the inevitable question: "Do you think you could buy me another one?"

How could I not? I groaned, head in hands.

When Finn and his mates weren't in town skating, they would sit at the computer and watch videos of people doing hair-raising skateboard stunts. One of these was called an ollie, defined on one website as: 'an aerial skateboarding manoeuvre in which board and skater lift off the ground together'. This involved skating to a spot at the top of a staircase and jumping. From there the aim was to fly mid-air at the same speed as the skateboard. Once you reached the bottom you landed on the board and skated away effortlessly, as though you always knew you would. The room for error was vast.

Raucous laughter would erupt at the sight of someone having a minor spill, utterances of empathy for the more serious incidents. I looked on occasionally, staring in horror at videos of young boys landing mid-way on a flight of stairs and skidding down, or crashing at the bottom, skateboard still in the air. Worst were the accidents when skating down rails of steps. This was called 'grinding the rail'. The aim was to ride your board along a staircase rail from top to bottom, land on the footpath and keep going. Often, instead of gliding down impressively, the skate boarder would end up with one leg either side of the rail, thus possibly endangering his prospects of reproduction in the future.

They also watched YouTube videos of arguments between skaters and those who objected to skateboarding in public places. Incidents were often filmed on somebody's phone as proof of what had happened, sometimes just for amusement, then posted on the internet. In true teenage style, video titles showed whose side the person filming was on: 'Psycho woman attacks skaters', 'Crack-head lady V skaters', 'Man and annoying girl yelling at skaters'.

"Hey, Mum, get a load of this guy, willya?"

Craig and Finn were watching a video showing a man laying down the law to a group of skaters. They'd found a church with a perfect set of stairs to ollie off. At first, it seemed he was protecting the church, but it soon became obvious he wasn't. He swore about the church, God, and in the same style, ranted aggressively at the young guys. This bloke was not interested in backing off. In fact, he shaped up to one of them.

"I'm glad we moved to the country instead of staying in Melbourne," I said.

"But there's some rad skate parks in Melbourne," said Craig reminiscently.

"I guess there are. But there's lots more people like this freak as well," I said, pointing to the man who still had not calmed down.

The man had made the skaters leave, accusing them of being dope dealers just because they had skateboards. He went after the guy he had been threatening, even though he was walking away and had his back to him. Luckily he decided it wasn't worth the trouble, but the key word was 'luck'.

I was becoming aware of the flak skaters copped when they were on footpaths, stairs or any raised areas that looked challenging. A young guy on one video was arguing with a man who was abusing him and his friends. The man was telling them to find another street to skate in, saying, "Go find a skate park or something."

"What skate park?" was the boy's reply.

That isn't to suggest teenagers only skated where they shouldn't because there was nowhere else. They also did it because they knew they weren't supposed to. Even so, a good skate park is a worthwhile addition to any town.

Finn and his mates would often come home with stories. "She went off her nut because we were skating too close to her shop."

Craig put in, "But there's nowhere to skate in Castlemaine. The council reckons there's a skate park. They call it a skate park, but it's hardly got anything."

"A mound of dirt next to the cricket pitch and a chair to sit on," Finn added.

The boys decided to do something about it.

*F*inn came home in high spirits on the night of one council meeting.

"Muuuuuwww." Sheba wanted attention. As he bent down to pick her up, he said, "We told them we thought there should be better facilities at the skate park."

"What did they say?"

"They told us plans are being drawn up to make a new skate park with two ramps, some steps, three mounds for bikes and seats around it."

"Awesome!" Finn looked at me dubiously. It wasn't cool for a parent to use teenage vernacular. "Well, it *is* awesome! What else did they say?"

"They want skaters from Castlemaine and surrounding areas to meet with them."

"Are you going to be one of them?"

"Yep." He looked proud of his achievement. "When it's finished, they're going to hold a skating competition and they want us to judge it."

"Good on *you*!"

Finn and his mates did in fact get the chance to judge the skating competition. But, by then, Finn's interests were starting to change. His music teacher had given him an electric guitar he didn't need anymore. The introduction to Deep Purple's 'Smoke on the Water' is the first thing you get given when you start learning. Walking past his room one afternoon I heard the first tentative strains of:

E – G – A , E – G – B/A , E – G – A – G – E

I closed my eyes and listened as he repeated it.

He'd gotten music. Or music had gotten him.

Moshing to the Metal

How do you describe the pent-up energy of young men about to leave school, not knowing who they are yet, but thinking they do? What do you allow them? What do you put your foot down about? What's a good way for them to get rid of all that testosterone-based drive without getting black eyes, losing teeth or getting young girls pregnant?

Heavy metal!

The answer to so many teenage boys' excess energy, the solution to so many parents' fears on Friday and Saturday nights. Were they out stealing cars? Doing drugs? Hanging around on street corners? They were not. They were at band practice or doing gigs.

Some say Jesus is coming back; who cares? Verily, let me say unto you that Jimi Hendrix has returned and is among us this very day. Hallelujah and praise the Electric Guitar. Maternal bias? Of course that was part of it. But he was a natural and had progressed in leaps and bounds since 'Smoke on the Water'. A reasonable version of the solo from *Paranoid* on my acoustic was the best I had managed.

They called themselves The Psychos. Craig, who had started growing his hair, played bass. Jake, another new mate of Finn's, had a drum kit with a double-kick, which meant any beat could be played at twice the speed. Practice happened at Jake's parents' house because they were so far out of town and couldn't possibly disturb anyone. Sam, a shy, self-contained boy, was lead singer. He was the right choice because of his already deep voice. They made an aggressive, hard-core mixture of grunge and death-metal.

Since Finn had explained that Wikipedia was not a band but a computer website, I had used it regularly. I typed in 'death metal' and pressed Enter. According to Wikipedia, death metal was a 'subcultural form of heavy metal with deep growling vocals, screams and fast double-kick drumming'. Thankfully, death metal singers did not sing/scream about necrophilia, Satanism, rape, mutilation, etc. It was not glam metal (the ones who wear make-up) or black metal (the ones who *do* sing about necrophilia, etc.) or doom metal. I decided I didn't want to know anything about doom metal and closed the web page.

It was no surprise that Finn had gone down this path. In my youth I had been to metal concerts that had made my ears ring for days. Before Finn was even born, I would play AC/DC and he would kick. Perhaps it disturbed him. Perhaps it woke him up. Or perhaps he was a head-banger before he'd even uttered his first cry. I liked to imagine, however foolishly, that I had somehow been partly responsible.

*I*t was a Friday night. Carol and I were going out for tea. Sam and Finn had been to get fish and chips. Coming up the front steps, Sam started practising his vocals. As they walked into the kitchen/lounge he uttered a cry that sounded like a character from a horror movie. Apparently, as I had gleaned from Wikipedia, it was called a 'death growl'. No doubt they had wanted to scare the hell out of me.

"That's very nice, dear." I said, in what I hoped was a maternal tone of voice. "But how can you do that for a whole show? Doesn't it hurt your throat?"

"The trick is to sing while you're breathing in," he explained to me.

"I'll take your word for it. No, wait; let me see if I can do it …" It was meant to sound like someone possessed by the devil or gathering up all their energy to lift a car off someone. I cleared my throat.

"Aaaaaarrrrhh!" I coughed, feeling the scratch in my throat from just a few seconds of death metal vocalisation. "I think I'll stick to the community singing group."

Sam, however, seemed impressed. He reached for his phone and asked, "Could you do that again?"

"No way. You're not recording me doing that."

"Go on. Just once. That was really good. I wanna send it to someone. Go on." He and Finn were enthused.

"Oh alright. What harm can it do?" I cleared my throat again. "Aaaaaarrrrhh!"

He and Finn were grinning from ear to ear. Sam pressed the button on his mobile phone, sending my demonic utterances to God knows who. I never did ask.

Just then, Carol knocked on the door. I wondered if she had heard me. It seemed she had not as she called out, "Helloooo …"

"Come in. You didn't hear that did you?"

"Hear what?"

"I just got persuaded to sing grunge metal style."

"I know what heavy metal is, but what's grunge metal?" Carol wanted to know.

"It's when you scream instead of sing. I'll put some on for you to listen to."

"That's okay, I'll take your word for it." Yoga chants and mantras were more her style.

After dropping off Finn and Sam at Jake's for band practice, I went to find Carol at the pub, a short distance from Jake's parents' house. It was usually quiet, but tonight there was a band.

"They sound good. Will we go and listen to them when we finish this?" Carol suggested.

We finished our meal and went next door. Up-beat jazz was the best way to describe their music. After a few songs, they decided to change the mood. The lead singer, a middle-aged woman with long black hair, who reminded me of one of the witches in Harry Potter, announced, "Now, we're going to change the pace a little bit. This is a slow, romantic one; maybe a good one for ... couples?" She looked around the room enquiringly. Her eyes fell on Carol and me, resting there. It took us a second to register why. When we finally realised, we cringed and stepped further away from each other. It had spoiled the mood. We didn't stay much longer.

"*Couples*," I mimicked as we walked to the car. "Bloody presumptuous."

"Yes, it was presumptuous, wasn't it?" We had been friends for almost twenty years. We lived in a fairly open-minded town, but under that open-mindedness was the closed-mindedness of a society that can't understand why two people who hang out regularly are 'only' friends. How open-mindedness could be changed into closed-mindedness I wasn't quite sure, but it definitely happened. As we crossed the road, we inclined our ears. The boys had turned their amps up.

"There goes Sam." He was letting loose with a roar to go with a drum roll and some manic guitar sounds. It was the end of a song. Perhaps they weren't far enough out of town.

"Aren't you glad they don't practise in your lounge room?" Carol asked.

"Sure am. I don't think they have any laid-back songs – for *couples.*"

"Have they got any gigs yet?"

"Not yet, but there is one in the pipeline. And they've entered Battle of the Bands."

The flyer read:

"This competition is a great opportunity for local talent to step up and show the community what they can do."

"Muuuuuwww." Sheba didn't understand how rude it is to interrupt people when they're talking on the phone.

"When do we need to be there?" I asked Jake's Mum.

"Muuuuuwww, Muuuuuuuuuuw."

"Six-thirty. That's an hour before it starts. That way they've got time to get their equipment out, sign in and meet everyone."

"Alright …"

"Muuuuuwww." It was dinner time.

"Be quiet. Not you, it's Sheba. She wants food. So, bring Jake here tomorrow. We can all go from here."

"Okay, see you at 5.30?"

"Sounds good. See you then. Isn't this exciting?"

Our metal head boys were through to the second last round of Battle of the Bands.

"Muuuuuuuuuuuuuuuuwww."

Sheba didn't share our excitement.

I've always found Maryborough a friendly town. But some of the comments that rang out over the music that night were far from welcoming. There are some people who seem to believe that, if it's not AC/DC then it's not music. Not that I had anything against Australia's best rock band. I just hoped the audience members at the back would not put the boys off.

"Get off the stage, ya fuckin' dickheads!" yelled a young inebriated man. Psychos hadn't even started playing yet. I was glad they didn't seem bothered. I looked to see if Jake's Mum was as shocked as I was.

"I don't get it," I said. "What do they want? Beethoven?"

"I don't think so."

"No. Saying 'Beethoven' around here is more like swearing than what they're saying,"

"Yes … Hey, they're starting."

The cymbals crashed '4-3-2-1' and any semblance of calm was blown sky-high as their guitars played in low-tuned, menacing tones. Battle of the Bands venues were alcohol free, but that didn't stop the more recalcitrant members of the public from smuggling it in. The more beer was consumed, the more vocal they became. It didn't deter the boys. There were far more people enjoying their performance, arms in the air, fingers making the devil's horn sign that was the equivalent of a thumbs-up in the heavy metal world. Some moshed as our boys did their set.

For those who do not know, 'moshing' is a way of showing your appreciation for hardcore heavy metal. You throw your head forwards in time with the music: a more violent version of head-banging.

They were well into their set. Finn and Craig were standing close to each other. They started to mosh while Finn played a guitar solo backed by Craig's bass, an impressive achievement in itself. Not realizing how close together they were, their heads collided. One can only imagine their utterances at that point. Those of us close enough to the stage didn't have to imagine. It was as obvious as when a football player goes for that crucial, game-clinching goal and misses.

They won the Maryborough heat, in spite of disparaging comments and the headaches Finn and Craig had inflicted on each other.

If you have long hair, moshing is particularly impressive. Dean had hair down past the waistband on his jeans. He was a regular at their gigs and moshed with the best of them.

I tried it once. On that occasion, the boys were booked to play at a pub. The 5-Flags Hotel hadn't had a band play there for years. The young music clientele started to trickle in as the dinner crowd trickled out. There would be two bands that night, Psychos and the support band, whose name I wasn't sure of. A group of people my age was sitting at a table near the back of the room.

"Anna!"

"How are you?"

"Alright thanks. What about you?"

"Good."

"Here to see Finn?"

"Of course," I said enthusiastically.

"Mother's pride and joy; it's written all over your face."

"Can I sit with you?"

"Sure."

The lead singer of the support band screamed her way into our memory banks. After their set, she smashed a perfectly good acoustic guitar on the edge of the stage.

"God," I said with my head in my hands.

"That's their style," said someone at our table, grinning at my reaction.

"You mean like when the Melbourne Symphony Orchestra finishes a concert and they all line up to bow?"

"That's right! Bowing is the Symphony Orchestra's signature way of saying thank-you." As he pointed to the stage, he added, "And that's theirs."

Hers more like it, I thought to myself. Out loud I said, "I get it. But would someone in the symphony orchestra smash one of their custom-made violins on the stage?"

They all liked that idea. I couldn't believe it. But then, what did I know? Maybe I was becoming an old fogey. It just seemed pointless. A kid could have started something that changed their life with that very guitar. I didn't press the issue.

After an interval, the boys we'd all been waiting for appeared in their standard jeans and flannel shirts (sleeves cut off in order to expose any muscle or tattoos that may have started to appear).

"Wooo-ooooo!"

Whistles and applause.

"Sick!"

"Yeah!"

Guitar tuning, people tapping microphones.

"Two-two-two."

Jake tested out the double-kick on his drum kit.

"Hey, how yez all doin'? We're gonna play you some metal now." The audience indicated their enthusiasm, and Sam joined in with a demonic utterance. "We've got our CD here as well," he said, pointing to a table at the side of the stage.

Finn punched out some chords on his guitar to warm up. Jake did one last test on the drums. I remembered the gigs I'd been to when I was his age: the volume, the people, the power of 'The Metal'. And there was my boy up there playing it.

"You ready, guys?" Sam and Jake nodded to each other. Four beats of the cymbals and he launched into the song – a long scream like an ancient warrior on horseback charging at the enemy. There were lyrics, but he was screaming them rather than singing. You couldn't understand a lot of it, but that wasn't the point. It wasn't mellow dinner-music.

Someone leaned closer to me so I could hear them "Have you had input into any of this?"

"Finn's been listening to heavy metal since before he was born," I said proudly.

I wanted to dance. Not just because it was them, but because they were good. We all got up from the 'olds' table and made our way to the dance floor. I'd washed my hair the day before and hoped this added to the spectacle of the middle-aged mother moshing to the metal.

The song ended. Someone asked, "What did Finn think of that?"

"Don't know. I didn't look. Didn't dare."

Get a Real Job

Moshing had given me a sore neck. It was also time spent unproductively. At least I was sure the employment workshop convener I would soon meet would think so.

Finn had slowly but surely been mutating into a teenager and was about to turn sixteen. It was a new time of life for both of us. He was finding his own feet, and I was preparing to make myself employable.

As part of sweeping changes to Australian society back in the seventies, Gough Whitlam's government had introduced the Sole Parent Pension. The cut-off date for receiving it had been set at the youngest child's sixteenth birthday. This meant you could concentrate on the job at hand – parenting.

Although I'd done jobs here and there, I hadn't been required to look for full-time work while I brought him up. But things were changing. New criteria were being implemented by the Howard government that meant sole parents would be required to look for work when their youngest child turned eight. The government justified this, in part, by citing those sole parents who apparently kept having children in order to stay on benefits. I wasn't sure what proof they had for this, but even if it were true, I didn't imagine too many people went to such lengths. An article in *The Age* explained the imminent changes.

> *"From July 2006, those sole parents new to the system will lose their right to the parenting payment once their youngest child turns eight. Instead, they will be placed on a Newstart allowance, which is twenty dollars less, and be required to look for a minimum of fifteen hours work a week. The Newstart allowance has a more stringent income test which means any extra money earned will cut their benefit."*

It seemed we were entering a new era. The work-or-be-damned philosophy was creeping back into society. Bringing Finn up on my own had meant I'd been extremely busy and had not noticed it happening.

A few days after the article appeared, someone wrote to *The Age* expressing his bewilderment at Mr Howard's attitude to sole parents. He said the approach being taken by the government to 'help' was to make things even more difficult for us. I was inspired to respond.

"Good on ya Mum." Finn was reading the letter I'd written in response, which *The Age* had seen fit to print.

"WORK THAT MATTERS

Thank you, Mr. C, (Letters 21/6) regarding recognition of parents' work. I only hope people continue to recognise the efforts we make without taking it for granted in the face of conservative trends in thought. Fairly soon I will have to seek employment and smile sweetly when confronted by the 'parents aren't workers' mindset. I wonder what chance I and others in my position have? 'So, you haven't worked for the past sixteen years? Hmmm.'

Having a well-adjusted, caring, responsible son or daughter is taken for granted. But this does not happen just because you want it to. You have to <u>work</u> to make it happen, in amongst washing, cleaning, shopping, chauffeuring, etc.

It is the most important job you can do and the most fulfilling. But just because it comes from instinct and caring, do not for one moment suggest it isn't work."

This effort even earned me a peck on the cheek from my cool-dude *(well-adjusted, caring)* adolescent son.

Now that I was on unemployment benefits, I went to job-class. I'd been a stay-at-home mum for sixteen years and was not ashamed of it, even though it was no longer politically correct to say so.

During our three-month course, we were handed out reams of paper telling us how to write résumés and application letters, how to present them to prospective employers, how to dress for interviews, what to say and what not to say. In the mornings we went around town giving résumés to businesses we thought we'd like to work for. In the afternoons we had to share our experiences with the class.

This particular afternoon, the convener had on a garishly coloured top. She wore those rectangular glasses that were coming into fashion at the time. The frames were almost as thick as the glasses themselves. I couldn't imagine how a person could see out of them. She spoke as though she was yelling across a paddock, and I longed for the session to be over. It was my turn to 'share'. Who had I given my résumé to? Had I received any encouraging responses?

"What was the most positive response you had today, Anna?" she enquired.

I thought back to the expressionless faces I'd encountered that morning and said, "None that spring to mind." It was true.

"Oh well, you'll get back into the swing of things. You've been unemployed for a long time, haven't you? It can take a while to get into that mindset," she said in her high-pitched voice. I started to speak, knowing I should keep silent but unable to stop myself.

"I haven't been unemployed."

"Oh?" She was interested all of a sudden.

"I've been doing the most important job there is: bringing up my son. I certainly haven't been idle." I looked into her face to find the smallest bit of acknowledgement for what I had said. There was none. She'd heard it all before. It wasn't exactly a roll of her eyes I saw, but a very slight movement of the head in order to look elsewhere and a thinning of the lips. I didn't tell her the most positive feedback I'd had recently was from people answering my advertisement for cash-in-hand gardening. That would have created a mixed response to say the least. Especially if I told them I'd accepted the work and was confident of getting more. Such flagrant destruction of the Australian economy could not be condoned under any circumstances.

On the walls, they'd pinned up A4 pieces of paper with sayings printed in black and white on them, such as:

'POSITIVE ATTITUDE,
POSITIVE RESULTS.'
and …
'IF IT IS TO BE,
IT'S UP TO ME.'

It was almost time to go home. I needed to go to the supermarket and also get petrol for the jerry can. I had a mowing job lined up the next day. *If it was to be, it was up to me!*

When I got home, the light on the answering machine was flashing.

"You have one new message," it said.

"Hello, this is Betty Hall. I was hoping you might be able to come and do a bit of gardening for me, a couple of hours every month. I'm getting a bit long in the tooth these days, and I need some help. You've got my number. Could you give me a call? Thank you."

"End of messages."

Meanwhile, despite living in a town without a lot of work, Finn never seemed to have trouble finding it. His first job was at the Two-Dollar Shop in town. I was keen to find a legitimate reason to go and see him at his first job.

"I thought I'd change this kitchen lino," I told Emma. "Some of that black and white checkered stuff would look good. I know where I can get some."

"Where?"

"The place Finn works."

The TV was on in the lounge, but we had not been watching it. Scenes of brawling were being shown on the news.

"Why can't they put some good stuff on the news for a change?" asked Finn as he walked past. "It's always stuff like this." He stopped to see what we were now looking at.

"The beach-side suburb of Cronulla in New South Wales saw rioting and violence today as tensions between Lebanese and white youths of the area boiled over," the ABC newsman told us, "in what was described by police as racially-based mob attacks. More than a hundred people were arrested and charged." Ian Henderson's voice deepened slightly as he continued, "Several people were stabbed, including one ambulance officer and a member of the police force."

"Hmmm."

"Glad we moved to the country," I said.

Finn looked at me as if I didn't get it.

"What?"

"There are idiots like that in the country too, Mum. I saw a guy pull a knife on someone the other night."

"You're joking. Where?"

"Outside the supermarket."

"Since when has stuff like that been happening in Castlemaine?"

Finn shrugged his shoulders.

"How close were you? Did they see you? Who were they?"

"I don't know who they were. I've never seen them before."

"So this is what's happening to our town. I don't like the idea of you being around stuff like that."

"You want me to stay home every night? 'Cos it's not gonna happen, Mum," he said.

"No, of course not. It's just a surprise to know things like that happen around here," I said as I gave him a protective hug.

"Yeah, yeah, okay Mum," he said as he went to the fridge.

"The place has certainly changed in twenty years," said Emma.

"Seems that way," I replied. "And my boy is out there in it, and

I just have to let it happen." I felt a sinking feeling, a worldwide parental phenomenon, I was sure. 'My boy'. I looked over at him making himself a snack. *He mustn't have heard me refer to him as a boy.* He didn't like to be called that anymore.

At the front of the shop was a display of viscous, sugar-filled lollies where kids could see them from the street. The lino was at the back of the store, and there he was, stamping price tags onto boxes and packing them on shelves.

"Excuse me, can I have some help, please?" I said, as if I didn't know him from Adam.

"What can I help you with today?" he said courteously, as if he didn't know me either. The cheeky grin almost started, but he managed to stop it.

"I want some lino, that black and white checkered design like they have in kitchens." He knew this of course. He'd heard me going on about it.

"Lino's over here," he said, pointing. I inspected the rolls of lino that were hanging horizontally one above the other. The one I wanted was almost all gone. It seemed everyone else had thought it was trendy as well.

"What a shame. Are they going to get any more in?"

"No, they're not getting any more of that one. Sorry."

"Hmm," I said, disappointed. "I'd set my mind on it." He didn't need to be told that either.

"Umm ... I'll have a look at these other ones."

"Okay, tell us if you want any help. I've got to get back to what I was doing."

"No worries. I'll let you know when I've made up my mind," I told him.

He grinned, knowing how long that would take.

"I'll just be over there," he said.

This one's too dark ... that's too elaborate ... yuck that's horrible ...

maybe this one …

"Could I get two meters of this one, please?"

"Yep, I can cut some of that for you in a jiffy," he said positively. "Just need a Stanley knife, won't be long."

In a jiffy, I said to myself under my breath as I watched him go into the back room. Nobody said that anymore. Uncle Jim must have taught him. I wondered how he was going.

Er ...

Castlemaine High had once been a technical college where students could learn a trade. But at some point, it had been forced to abandon most of the 'tech' subjects it offered. It was now a more mainstream high school, offering more standard type classes. Finn was a hands-on, practical person. He was not academically inclined but went to school because he knew he had to. Even that stopped being enough after a while.

"Come on, get out of bed!"

"Er ..."

"Finn, you have to go to school. You can't just lie there all morning."

"Er ..."

"I guess 'er' is better than telling me to piss off."

"Er ..."

"Get UP!"

This was a new phase in his teenage development. *'Er'* seemed to be the standard answer to anything asked of him before ten in the morning. Other parents had told me similar things, or nodded their heads in empathy when I had described Finn's disposition lately. I was discovering that all teenage boys have two things in common, especially as their adolescence progresses; they talk in monosyllabic grunts until they've been up for at least an hour, and their feet smell incredibly bad. Both aspects of his being were obvious that morning.

"This isn't healthy," I said, as I sat down at the end of his bed. "If you aren't getting your work done, bring it home and I'll help you with it if I can," I told him. A string of expletives and something about me leaving him alone followed.

"I called Uncle Jim yesterday. I told him how you're having trouble in the mornings and he *wants* you to get out of bed and do something with your time. He's finding it more and more difficult to do that himself. If you won't go to school, let's go and see him today."

"Er ... Okay. Just let me wake up ..."

"I'll call him and let him know we're coming."

"I'll be teaching you to do this soon," I told him as we drove along the freeway.

"Cool."

"You'll have to have some professional lessons too. Just to make sure I've taught you all the right things ..."

"Like what the speed limits are?" I drove like a snail.

"Smart-arse."

"Mum, the way you drive, you might as well get out and walk."

"I'm not *that* slow."

"At least you play good music in the car." He had lent me his Metallica CD for this journey, which had been a bit like a doctor lending you their stethoscope.

Uncle Jim was sitting on his front porch. He was getting older all the time and it was starting to show in his gait and the lines on his face.

"Look at you, Finn! When did that happen?" he asked, referring to all the changes in appearance Finn had been through since the last time they saw each other.

Shyly, he smiled and gave Uncle Jim a quick hug.

We drank tea and talked for hours. He told us he was going to be staying at a nursing home in Castlemaine that he had been on the waiting list for.

"At least you'll be closer to us."

During our visit he mentioned things more than once and needed to be reminded of people's names. Finn and I exchanged looks each time he did it, aware of the change that had started happening. I hoped it might at least be a wake-up call for Finn; a reminder that he *could* get up in the morning and *should*. His life was just beginning.

He might not have been moving in leaps and bounds at school, but Finn had a job three afternoons a week. It wasn't NASA headquarters, but he worked, and they paid him. He had bought a T-shirt with money he had saved. It had the word Fuck emblazoned on it which, of course, was the reason he bought it. At least now he was motivated to go to school.

I certainly hadn't been willing to buy it for him. I'd been happy to buy him a 'Metallica – Kill 'Em All' T-shirt. Any metal-head worth their surround sound system will tell you that Metallica is one of the most important bands of the metal genre called 'thrash'. *Kill 'Em All*, the title of one of their albums, wasn't the most wholesome concept, but at least it wouldn't attract the police's attention.

"You can't wear that to school!"

"I'm going to school. You said you wanted me to go to school. I'm going to school," he replied.

"Oh fuck!" I groaned hypocritically.

"Chill out, Mum," he said, his voice taking on an air of annoyance.

"So, you're gonna stand there and tell me that wearing a T-shirt with profanities on it to school is what everyone does …" I threw my hands in the air and walked towards the kitchen. *He's loving every minute of this*, I thought.

It was a trade-off. I was meant to bask in the relief of him going to school for the first time in a month and ignore what was written on his T-shirt. Teachers were the other ones who were meant to ignore a message that was probably directed at them. They were supposed to just receive it without saying anything; in his version of an ideal world anyway. Mine too, if I was really honest about it. If all his teachers were like the one I had spoken to at parent-teacher night, I didn't blame him. At least he hadn't lost his spirit. That was more important than any retribution that might be coming his way. He tossed his backpack over his shoulder and made for the front door.

"Seeya," I said, shaking my head.

An hour later, there he was coming up the front steps.

"What happened?"

"Headmaster saw the T-shirt, told me to go home and change it," he said in a monotone.

"Well gee, I wonder *why*," I said, rolling my eyes. "What did you expect?"

"It's a T-shirt."

"With offensive language on it."

"It doesn't say *anything!*"

"Oh, yes it does," I replied.

"Not like you don't say it," he retorted. He had me there.

"Yes, that's true. In that case, change your fuckin' T-shirt and fuckin'-well get back to fuckin' school," I said in the calmest tone of voice I could manage.

"I'm going to make a coffee first," he informed me as he made his way to the kitchen area. I thought I saw the beginnings of a grin on his face. I was glad he wasn't afraid to push the boundaries. But I couldn't let myself show it.

"I'll have one too – white, one sugar. Then you *get back to school.*"

"Yeah, I know, Mum. I'll get something to eat on the way. You got five bucks?"

"Yes, Finn, I've got five bucks. But only if you change that T-shirt."

He made a noise indicating primal frustration and went to his room to change. After the coffee, he went back to school.

I'm out of my depth, I thought to myself as I sat on the purple couch. A feeling of helplessness came over me.

"Muuuuuwww."

"I don't want to take up smoking again, do I?" I asked Sheba as I picked her up.

"Muuuuuwww."

"No, of course I don't."

The last seventeen years had been an endless succession of:
- cooking
- cleaning
- painting rooms
- putting bandaids on wounds
- defrosting fridges
- vacuuming
- pulling up carpets
- wallpapering
- collecting firewood
- chopping it
- scrounging in op-shops
- going to garage sales
- gardening
- arguing
- comforting
- listening
- driving
- babysitting
- shopping
- replacing tap washers
- sitting on washing machines that stopped on the spin-cycle
- taking trailer loads to the tip
- mowing lawns
- doing other people's gardens
- cleaning their houses.

I had loved all of it, motivated by the knowledge that, no matter what else I did in life, it was the most important thing I would ever do. And despite rude T-shirts and other provocative behaviour, he was growing up to be a very nice young man.

When, at about seven or eight, he had started wanting expensive things like his mates had, I couldn't always give them to him. But I could tell him I loved him every day of his life. I had taken a silent vow to do just that.

But now he wasn't far off twenty. He didn't need to hear that, he knew it already, it embarrassed him. What he needed was male influence, a mentor, someone he could trust, confide in, ask those personal questions he would never dream of asking me. Uncle Jim was in care at a hostel and was losing his memory. He would have given Finn all the advice and healthy male influence necessary. But he was no longer in a position to.

A wave of guilt came over me, knowing it had been my choice to get involved with John all those years ago. But if I had not, Finn would not exist. To have a child with someone whom I knew, deep down inside, would not stay around, was the most stupid thing I had ever done. But regret was not an option. There was no point beating myself up about decisions I had made as a clueless young woman.

After years of getting it all done without a man, here was something I could not do; no matter how hard I tried, I couldn't be a father.

First Time for Everything

*I*t seemed I wasn't the only one who'd been thinking of taking up smoking. Finn had been going for what he described as a 'walk around the block' with one of his mates for almost a week before I cottoned on.

It was only one smoke in the open air. A quick trip to the toilet – nobody could stop you from doing that – gave him the opportunity to brush his teeth while he was in there. But I hadn't lost my sense of smell. This time I was waiting. The front door opened and in he walked.

"Hello! I haven't given you a hug yet today." I put my arms around him before he had the chance to protest.

"Ah, yeah. Hi, Mum," he said suspiciously. I put my nose into the thick mess of hair and breathed. It was cigarette smoke, no doubt about it.

"Have you started smoking?"

"Why ask me when you know the answer?"

"You've been smoking. I don't care how I say what. How long have you been doing it?"

"A week."

"That's what the walk around the block is?"

"Yeah, Mum," he answered resignedly. Then the rebellious tone returned. "I'm not going to stop. I can buy them with money from my pay left over after I pay my share of the rent."

"Yes, I know you can. You'll get them whether I want you to or not. Shit."

I walked to the kitchen, turned to face him and said angrily, "Don't Do Drugs. Do you hear what I'm saying to you?" I took him by the shoulders and looked straight into his eyes.

"It's okay, Mum. I'm not going to do drugs." he answered.

"*Don't.*"

I was on the couch when he came out of the bathroom.

"Now that I've finished being annoyed with you …"

"… you wanna talk about it," he said, finishing my sentence.

"Exactly. I wanna know why. Why now?"

"Stress. Because of school mostly."

"School. I thought it might be. It's no use telling you that kids your age, only a few hundred years ago, had to leave school whether they wanted to or not? So they could have the 'privilege' of working a twelve-hour day in a woollen mill or something?"

"Uh no, Mum. It wouldn't!"

"If there's ever a documentary on work conditions of the past, we should watch it together."

"It's not just school. It's life in general."

"What? Girls? Social life? Sexual stuff?"

"No, no, Mum!" He didn't like me even mentioning such things. "It's just life."

"Are you happy?"

"Yeah. Not jumping out of my skin, but okay."

"Not depressed?"

"No, Mum, don't worry!"

"I'm your mum. Of course I worry, especially at this age. Teenage years are notoriously difficult." He grinned at this.

I put my arm around his shoulders and kissed him on the head. The smell of smoke was still in the mess of hair.

"You're a good mum."

"Thanks, luv."

"The way you're talking to me right now makes me feel like an adult."

"Good."

"And I'm not gonna do drugs, Mum."

"You don't want to end up like Barry. Do you?"

That made him stop and think. Barry was someone we knew who had overdone things a bit.

"No, Mum. I do not. Not at all."

"No. You certainly don't. And about school. You're not stupid. It might seem like the teachers think you are, but you're not."

"I know, Mum."

"Do you really? They're teachers. You might tell yourself you don't care what they say, but they're making judgements about you. It's part of their job. And if you don't perform well at the particular things they teach, they have to give you a low mark. But we all have things we're good at and things we're not."

"I'm not good at much."

"That is *not* true. There used to be a tech school in Castlemaine, where you could learn trades – woodwork, metalwork, bricklaying, building. But they closed that part of the school down. So now you have to stick your head in a book all day, and that's not what you're best at. That does not mean you're stupid. It means you're not academic. Big difference."

"I never thought of it like that."

"Maybe you've been too busy trying not to think about it at all 'cos it's bothering you?"

"Yeah, I guess so." The cheeky grin appeared for a second.

"You're a hands-on person. Like me. Like my Dad. Like Uncle Jim."

He seemed to have gotten some reassurance from what I'd said. I saw it in his face. I didn't think it would be enough to stop him from smoking, but I could see I'd made an impression.

"And one of these days, you might discover something you love to study and read about. When I say you're not academic, I mean that's not where you're at now. But things can change. I don't know. You don't know."

The idea of taking up smoking seemed to be hanging in the air like a bad smell. Some of Finn's mates had started around this time. Dean and Max were brothers and were often at our place. One night there were five of them in Finn's room watching a video, eating pizza and drinking Coca Cola. They were relaxing into the night, sprawled over Finn's bed and sitting against the wall. All of them had their socks off, their organic-smelling sneakers strewn around the floor.

"Jeeesus! Can't you open a window in here or something?"

"Muumm! Take a chill pill."

"I don't need a chill-pill. I need a gasmask."

"That's really funny," he said in a dead-pan voice.

"Anyhow," I said, pretending to choke, "I just put the kettle on. Came in to see if any of you wanted a cuppa."

"Yeah. Thanks, Mum."

"Yeah, I'll have one. Thanks …" Max said. His mates often left my name hanging in the air, unsure what to call me. I wasn't *Mrs* McAllister. They weren't sure about Miss or Ms, or Anna. And, of course, I wasn't 'Mum'. The rest of them declined a drink, but about half an hour later, Dean came out to get himself some water.

"Hey, where are the glasses?"

"Cupboard above the stove."

"Thanks."

He smelt of tobacco. Since when had he been a smoker? It turned out he wasn't. He had just smoked his first cigarette in Finn's room and his second, third and fourth, as I would be told later. I went back to what I had been doing at the computer. There was a crash.

I turned around to see Dean on the floor. He was having a seizure right there in my kitchen.

"Hey! Finn! Get out here now, I'm not joking!"

By the time Finn and the other boys came out of his room, Dean was sitting up. He was disoriented but no longer convulsing.

We got some cushions and put him on the purple couch.

"The same thing happened to our dad when he had his first cigarette," Max told us.

"Oh well, that makes it alright then," I said dryly. "Hey, Dean, do you know where you are?"

"Yeah. What the …"

"You had a fit, mate. Have you ever had one before?"

"No."

"Only get up when you're ready. Stay there as long as you need to."

"I'm okay," he said. I frowned. How could he be? It took me days to recover from one of these things.

"Will you make an appointment to see the doctor?" I asked him.

"She'll be right, I'm fine," he said as he got up, shook himself and headed back to Finn's room.

"You sure you're okay?" I asked.

"Yep, fine," he said.

"Are you sure?"

"Yeah."

It was unbelievable. Boys that age seem to be immune from just about anything. No wonder they think themselves invincible.

My fear of the internet was well and truly gone. Once they went back to Finn's room, I looked up 'cigarettes and epileptic seizures'. One website told me that cigarettes can cause seizures in people with no epileptic indications, as had just happened with Dean. It also informed me that epileptics who smoke are more at risk of having seizures than those who don't. But, as well as that, epileptics who wanted to *give up* smoking were at risk of seizures too. Tobacco could be 'anti-convulsant', like the medicines I took, or 'pro-convulsant'.

I certainly wouldn't be taking up smoking again, no matter how stressful things became.

*F*inn and his mates were doing all sorts of things for the first time: thinking seriously about careers, getting drunk, getting work, smoking cigarettes, staying out late, learning to drive, taking exams, falling in love. For his generation, falling in love was, more often than not, linked with spending the night together as well. Some things are the same throughout history. But his generation wasn't worried about hiding the facts, even from parents.

It seemed Finn had fallen in love with a girl named Celine. I was starting to see her at our place a lot more. She had become part of the group. She was a year older than Finn, had her licence and a car. That meant she could get herself home whenever she wanted to. One particular night, it seemed she was in no hurry to leave. I was in bed reading. She came into my room and sat on the end of the bed.

"What are you reading?" she asked me.

"*The Book Thief*. It's about a girl who lives in Germany in the time of World War Two. She steals a book from one of the burnings the Nazis used to do. You know they did that?"

"They burned anything that didn't agree with their point of view."

"That's right. So she starts making a habit of stealing/rescuing books. As well as that, her family is hiding a Jewish boy in their basement so the Nazis don't find him. It's a really good book. I can't put it down."

"I like reading, too." She had a quiet way about her. I presumed parental approval still meant something, even with the social changes that had taken place since I was a teenager. If this was to be Finn's first girlfriend, I approved.

We talked for a little while longer before she went and made some coffee. Were they hoping to stay up until sunrise? And if so, what would they do to fill in the time? I had a feeling I knew.

My suspicions were confirmed next morning. I looked up from the kitchen bench as they both came into the room. Had they or had they not? If the coy smiles on their faces meant anything, they had. There was no point expecting them to wait until they got married, not anymore. Nevertheless, I was taken aback.

"T ... tea? Coffee maybe?"

"No thanks, Mum. But can Celine have a towel? She's got to go soon."

"Yes, of course. They're in the big cupboard in there," I said. She went into the bathroom. Finn sat at the desk.

"What are you looking at me like that for, Mum?"

"Like what?" I couldn't keep the smirk off my face. "Oh well, it had to happen sooner or later, didn't it?"

"Yeah, whatever, Mum. Whatever!" He had gone all shy, not to mention red. He wanted it to be okay with me, but he didn't want to talk about it. My religious upbringing turned somersaults in my head as I processed this new, unspoken information. I was becoming more conservative in middle age.

"I'm glad you're happy. But don't you go becoming a father yet. Right?"

"Muuum! She's just in there. She can hear every word you say."

"No she can't, the shower's going. I want you to look me in the eyes and tell me you'll be careful."

"Yes, Mum, of course," he said, as he stopped Sheba from jumping onto the table.

"There's no *of course* about it," I said, making the tea. "It only takes one time and your whole life could change forever." I went to the desk, gave him his tea, leant closer to him and said, "Look at me. Con...tra...*cep*...tion."

"Yeah, Mum. Okay, okay." I could tell by the look in his eyes I had made the point.

I had a new love in my life as well, but it was not a person. Gardening had become like oxygen. Getting my hands in the dirt was soul-restoring. The most expensive, fashionable fragrance on the market could not compare to the smell of water and earth together. Uncle Jim had seen the improvements I'd made to the front garden, but had not remembered encouraging me to do it.

We were in the middle of a heatwave, and nights were the time to be active. There was no other sound, an occasional car in the distance, the sound of someone talking, the hose. But there was another sound as well. I listened closer. The water was being sucked into the soil, small holes being made where it was softest. The ground was coming alive, showing its appreciation for the water, asking for more.

"Finn," I whispered. "Come out here!"

"What for?"

"Come on, just come out! Stand here and listen. Can you hear that?"

"What is it?"

"The ground is thirsty. It's drinking."

"That's really cool, Mum."

We Don't Need You

A short while after Finn and his mates had started their heavy metal band, I joined a folk band. I'd been playing washboard with folk musicians in jam sessions, but life had been too complicated for me to be in a band. Now that the epilepsy was under control, I could drive again. Finn was doing more of his own thing, so I had more free time. The band practised every Sunday at a pub just out of town. But Simon (the man who had come around on my fortieth and lit a joint in front of our neighbour) was about to change all that.

He had been acting a bit weird lately, or as some would have it, 'weirder than usual'. Even though we didn't have a band leader, he had decided we needed one, and there were no points for guessing who he thought should be appointed to that role. He had also started taking it upon himself to make rules, and everyone else had let him. However, there were raised eyebrows at some of the things he'd been coming out with. I had been told that sometimes he believed he was God. I was about to experience that firsthand.

It was the perfect day for a bike ride, especially with a music practice session at the end of it. I parked the bike and untied the washboard from the basket. Most of the band was already in the beer garden. I got some soda water and went to sit at a table. Simon approached and sat down opposite me.

"Anna," he said, the sound of a reproachful parent in his voice, "this band is restricted to certain types of musical instruments. We do not require percussion. You are not welcome here."

"Excuse me?" I said in astonishment. He was one of the people who had suggested I join.

"You are not welcome in this band. The presence of the devil is around you." A malevolent expression appeared on his face.

"The devil? How on earth did you come to that conclusion?" I hadn't yet cottoned on that he was serious.

He stood up and made a declaration. "I will not play in this band as long as this woman harasses me."

"Harass? What the …"

Stan, one of the fiddle players took me to the other side of the beer garden. "He's not very well at the moment, Anna. Haven't you noticed? You should go home."

"But I just rode my bike to get here. It took me an hour. You're telling me I have to turn around and go back?"

"When he gets like this, he's unpredictable."

"What do you mean?"

"He's not stable. You should go." He was serious.

"Leave? You're all just going to let him do this?"

"I know it sucks." Wendy, another member, had come over to us. "But you know what he's like."

"Er – no. I don't know what he's like. I've got no idea what you're talking about. This has come right out of the blue, being told I have the presence of Satan upon me? Will someone please tell me what's going on?"

These people had known him for decades. I was a relative newcomer. "You're just gonna let him walk all over you – oh, sorry, that's right, walk all over me. It's no skin off your noses, is it?"

"Just let things cool down for a bit and see what happens when he gets better," advised Stan.

"And when might that be?"

No answer, just stony stares. It was a good thing I loved bike riding.

After a long ride home, I went and told Ben and Lisa what had happened.

"I couldn't believe it," I told them. "They all just looked at me and didn't say anything. They just let him do it. So that's the last time they're going to see me."

"Darling one, I'm sorry he did that to you. Would you and Finn like to come around and have some dinner with us this evening?" asked Ben.

"Thank you, that would be lovely," I replied.

I went home and slumped on the purple couch. Sheba jumped up onto me to give comfort. Sometimes it was like she knew you needed it.

Carol and I were driving to Daylesford the following weekend. "So I get there and he sees me, and his face gets this expression like what-the-hell-is-she-doing-here, and he comes and tells me the band cannot help me," I told her. "No percussion required, thank you very much." I said in a pretend-posh voice.

Carol's reaction was completely out of character. "That misogynistic, psychopathic arsehole!" The lady someone had once described as having a 'nun-like disposition' had just ripped the guts out of someone with her words and done it better than I'd ever heard it done before.

"It was almost worth it happening just to hear you say that," I told her once I stopped laughing.

She was reconsidering her comment. "But then really he's more of a sociopath than a psychopath." Her composure had returned.

*M*y boy was starting to talk about leaving home. The future stretched out in front of me. A part of my life was coming to a close. What would it be replaced with? What would I do with myself once he wasn't living with me anymore? I didn't have a job. I couldn't even hold down a position in a band, it seemed. I was at my weekly visit to the job search consultant, telling her how pointless it felt.

"As soon as I tell them I'm epileptic, their faces fall. It's not the kind of thing you can hide." I corrected myself: "Once you start having a seizure, I mean. It's not something you can give up being, like a smoker."

"There are anti-discrimination laws in place to help people in your situation get work," the job-search woman told me.

"That's good." I wanted to believe her. But I didn't. Nobody was obliged to employ me if they didn't want to. And so far, nobody had wanted to. How long would I have to play the charade of confident job seeker? How was I meant to convince someone to employ me when there were a hundred non-epileptics in their twenties going for the same job? As far as the job-seek people were concerned, my lack of motivation meant there was something the matter with *me*. It wouldn't be an issue for much longer. I was about to become officially disabled.

Next Thing I Knew (3, 4, 5 & 6)

"How can I help you today, Anna?" my GP asked politely.

"I'm not sure how to describe it. It's not physical. I think I'm depressed. I don't know. That's what I've come to see you about."

"What makes you think you're depressed?"

"It's getting harder to get out of bed in the morning. I'm not coping. I cry. Not all the time, but more than ever before. I'm told I have to get a job. But I know damn well, no-one's going to hire me. The only way I'm going to get a job is if I move back to Melbourne, but I don't want to do that. Castlemaine is my home. All my friends are here … well, not quite as many as I thought I had."

"Why do you say that?" he wanted to know.

I told him about the folk band I'd just been kicked out of. "And everyone else just let him do it. Nobody stood up for me, not one single person. I thought I had friends in that band. I feel betrayed. And the worst thing is, my son's about to leave home. It could happen any day. He's said if he finds somewhere he will move."

"Do the two of you get along?"

"Yes. We get along very well. He's my best mate. That's the trouble.

When he leaves home, the gap that will all of a sudden be there after all this time ..." The tears were going to start if I didn't stop talking. "I've never felt so down. It's all getting a bit much."

"Well, from what you've told me, it does sound as though you aren't coping. Perhaps a course of Sertraline will help you get back on track," he said as he continued recording what I had said on the computer in front of him.

"Will Sertraline do anything to affect the Dilantin?" I asked him as he looked at his computer screen.

"There's a small degree of interaction, but nothing to worry about, I would think."

He sounded confident. He was the doctor. I went to get the prescription filled; even that made it seem like I was getting some control of my life back.

After taking the antidepressants for a fortnight, the sadness had disappeared. But so had the happiness. As I stood at the kitchen sink, I thought about the strange absence of feeling. It was like the reading on a heart monitor when someone has died: neither up nor down. At least I wasn't bursting into tears all the time.

"Mum, can you give me a lift out to Craig's?" Finn said as he hung up the phone. "He's got a few of us staying overnight."

"Sure. When do you need to go?"

"I'll just get a few things in my pack, yeah?"

"Okay, whenever you're ready," I said, thinking ahead to the evening. I didn't have anything planned. Maybe I would see about changing that. "You ready?"

"Yep."

It was a sunny Sunday afternoon with not a lot of traffic on the road. We were halfway to Craig's parents' house when it happened. The Feeling came over me. The last thing I remember was heading for a tree.

Next thing I knew, I was on the other side of the road sitting on the nature strip. There was a crowd milling around – police and people who had come out from the pub. There was a pub on this side of the road? This was the wrong side of the road to be driving on. Wasn't it? Why was I sitting there? Had I been driving?

There was the car, crumpled and being assessed by the police. *Police?*

Oh, not the car. Oh shit, not the car. And then I saw him standing with one of the police, talking, nodding his head and moving on to the next person. In charge.

"Finn? Oh my GOD!"

Had he been in the car with me? I had no recollection. Had I been driving him somewhere? Yes, I had. He came over to me and put his arm around my shoulder. "It's okay, Mum. Everything's okay." Then I lost consciousness again.

*N*ext thing I knew, I was sitting on the nature strip feeling dazed and confused. I had the sense that something bad had just happened, but I didn't know what. I also didn't know that I was continually losing and re-gaining consciousness as I was sitting there. Why was I sitting on the side of the road? It was something to do with driving. But I was on the wrong side of the road for that. I'd been driving too many years to forget which side of the road I was supposed to be on. There was a car, people looking at it, assessing the damage.

What the …?

And then I saw Finn with someone, talking and pointing to something across the road. The person put their arm around his shoulders. I should have been the one doing that. But I wasn't capable of doing anything except sitting there in a daze.

*T*hen I lapsed into the unknown again. Next thing I knew, I was sitting on the nature strip. There were people milling around nearby. Why were they here? Why was I here? Where was Finn? I needed to see him, to feel his arms around me.

"Finn?"

Then I saw the car. I'd crashed it. Finn was talking to someone and shaking his head, doing the little grin he got when someone said something foolish.

"Finn?"

He came and sat down on the grass with me, putting his arm around my shoulders.

"It's okay, Mum."

"What happened? Are you alright?"

"Yeah, I'm fine. Car's fucked though."

"What happened?"

"You had a fit."

"No!"

There was that little grin again. "Yes, Mum, you did."

Then I lost consciousness again.

The next thing I knew, I was still sitting on the nature strip. An ambulance had arrived. My shoulder was hurting.

What had happened? *Oh God, I've crashed the car.*

No.

The fit.

No!

There was Finn nodding to the police as they got back into their car.

"Finn!"

"Mum, it's alright, you'll be fine."

I stood up.

"But what about you?"

"I'm fine, Mum."

"I crashed the car."

"That's right, Mum. You had a fit."

"Oh God." It was sinking in. I held his hands in mine.

"There's a tow truck coming to take the car away, and they're sending you to Bendigo Hospital to X-ray your shoulder. You did something to it."

"It does hurt," I said rubbing it. "How are you getting home?" Going to Craig's had completely gone out of my head. Perhaps Finn had forgotten about it too.

As the paramedics took me by the arm and led me to the ambulance, Finn said "The police will give me a lift. I better go over." he said, pointing to their car.

"Yes, of course. I'll call you later. I need someone to pick me up from the hospital."

"Sure. Your address book is next to the phone. I'll call someone when I get home."

"Tell them to call Bendigo Hospital," the paramedic told Finn as I was being helped into the ambulance. "They'll let them know where your Mum is so they can come and get her." This was an all too familiar scenario.

"You'll have to go back to your specialist now, won't you?" Carol said as we got into her car.

"Yes I will. I thought everything was fine."

"It must be a constant source of worry, not knowing if or when it's going to happen again."

In Green Street, as we drove past the old houses and established trees, I saw that the old couple who'd extended their garden to the nature strip had another car parked in their driveway. The artist lady on the other side was still up; I could see the light on at her place. I could see the light on at our place too. The car wasn't parked outside. I sank in my seat as the reality hit home again.

"No car. What the hell am I going to do now? Ask Mum and Dad for money again?"

"You'll figure something out," Carol said.

"What I'm going to do now is go inside and give my son a hug and tell him how sorry I am. Are you coming in? I can make you a cup of tea."

"I'll come in for a while."

"Thank you for being there for me – again!"

"That's alright. You'd do the same for me," she said as she put her arm around my shoulder and walked with me.

Finn had phoned some mates and they were there. Kauri had Maori blood and an Afro. I had once tried to persuade him to grow it and colour it green. I had even offered to pay for the dye. He hadn't taken me up on it. The look on his face as he moved towards me was one of genuine concern. Craig was the same. Like Finn, they were both taller than me now. To wrap my arms around these skinny teenage boys was good medicine.

"I'm so sorry, Finn." Once again, he had the little grin, the amused but understanding laugh.

"You already *told* me that, Mum! It's o–*kay!*"

"But it's not. I could have killed you." I tried to push the thought away. "That could have been *you* in the hospital tonight."

"Well, you didn't. You'll find a way to get another car. You'll just have to not drive for a while." His voice was mature and controlled. Having a mother who had epilepsy was a lesson in composure.

"You got a lift home with the cops. Did the neighbours see?"

"Ha! They did, yeah. Les was worried. He came over and asked what was wrong. I told him, and he came and sat with me for a while."

"What a good man."

"Yeah, he sure is. Will you have to go back to the doctors now?" he asked.

"Yes, I'll have to go and see the specialist. I won't be able to drive there to see him … Oh God."

"Didn't you just start taking anti-depressants?" asked Carol. I sat down on the purple couch while she put the kettle on. "Do you think that's why it happened?"

The anti-depressants *had* interfered with the Dilantin levels in my bloodstream. I thought back to what the doctor said when he prescribed them – 'a small degree of interaction, but nothing to worry about' – except if you were one of those super-sensitive epileptics like me.

"What did they say about your shoulder?" Finn wanted to know.

"It's been put out of place. A bit of pain for a while, nothing they can do about it." I took his hand and put it on my shoulder so he could feel the bone that was now out of place.

"Eeeeuuw."

"And the Kingswood. All those years and now, bang!" I turned to Finn. "But we're okay." I settled into the purple couch. "By the way, how did we get onto the other side of the road?"

Finn knew exactly how it had happened. "I saw you start to go weird. So I reached over and grabbed the steering wheel and turned it so we didn't crash into the tree." The tree, the last thing I remembered seeing. He had saved our lives. "When it started you went like this …" he threw his head back and stretched his abs, planting his feet firmly on the ground to demonstrate. "Your foot was still on the accelerator, so we were going fast."

"I'm sorry." I grabbed his hand. "I'm sitting here going on about the bloody car and all the time you saved our lives. I'm a selfish bitch."

He held my hand tighter and looked at me. "Don't say things like that, Mum."

Carol chimed in as well. "Finn's right. Don't say things like that. You're being unfair on yourself."

I tried to believe it, to absorb what two of my best friends were telling me.

Later, in bed, I tried to ignore the pain. Paracetamol wasn't enough. If I lay on my right side, gravity would stretch the muscles in my left shoulder. If I lay on my left, the pressure was unbearable. The doona surrounded me with its warmth, but the pain was relentless, and I couldn't sleep. That, along with the thought, *if I don't sleep, I'll have a fit,* kept me awake for most of the night.

And so, next day I found myself being guided to the purple couch. I could hear their voices, comforting and gentle.

"You had another seizure, Anna," Ben informed me.

"Here, put this cushion behind her back." It was Lisa.

It can't have been severe. Nobody had to explain why they were there. I remembered that Carol had come over in the morning and that Ben and Lisa had dropped in as well. No doubt someone would put the kettle on. I sat back and allowed other people to take charge. Nothing more was required of me.

Dr Jenkins sat at his desk listening while I told him what had happened.

"Yes, your doctor definitely should've let me know he'd changed your medication. I'm starting to think the Disability Pension might be the best option for you," he told me.

"*Disabled*? I'm not disabled! I've got epilepsy, I'm not in a wheelchair," I said incredulously.

"Disability doesn't have to be visible," he reminded me. "Diabetes, for example; how do you know a person is diabetic unless they tell you or their sugar levels drop? But it certainly makes its presence felt in a person's life, doesn't it?"

"I never thought of it like that."

"Most people with epilepsy who take Dilantin can get away with lowering their dose by, say, a hundred milligrams with no problem. But some need to be extremely careful about maintaining their condition in terms of sleep, reduction of medication, and so on. I think you fall into that category."

"The disability pension. That means I won't have to go looking for work that doesn't exist?"

He gave a slight laugh. "I don't know, Anna. You'll have to talk to Centrelink about what they require from you."

"It would be a relief, not having to spend so much time looking for work that nobody wants to give you. The one job in Castlemaine I've ever had *offered* to me was driving taxis, and I had to say no. Ironic, isn't it? If you're allowed to have a licence at all you can drive yourself and your loved ones around. But you can't drive a complete stranger anywhere if you're being paid to do it." My specialist was sympathetic, but his time was limited. "What do I have to do?" I asked him.

"Go and see Centrelink. Tell them you want to be interviewed for eligibility. They'll arrange an appointment. I'll send you a letter to take with you when you go, giving them my opinion and asking them to transfer you over to the disability pension."

"Thank you. *Thank you.*"

"Centrelink may not agree with my recommendation," he warned. "But I'm reasonably sure from past experience they will."

I heard the motorbike. The postman had stopped at our letterbox. There was the letter from Centrelink. I sat on the steps and ripped open the envelope. They'd decided to pension me off. I put on the kettle, dialled the phone and waited.

"Your call is third in the queue."

"Your call is important to us."

"Your call is second in the queue."

"Please wait and someone will be with you shortly."

"Your call is …"

"Hello, how can I help you today?"

"Hello. I just rang because I've recently been put on the disability pe …"

"Could I have your customer reference number, please?"

"That won't be necessary. I just wanted to ring up and say …" I didn't know how to put it. "I've been on the phone plenty of times arguing with you people. So I thought if I can do that, I can ring up and say 'thank you' as well. What it means not to have to suck up to people who aren't going to give you a job anyway is more than I can express in words. Like I said, thank you."

"Well, that's quite alright," said the woman. "I'm glad we've been able to be of some assistance." I thought I heard something in her voice that sounded like she'd been pleasantly surprised.

"*It*'s because of the change in the medicine that this accident even happened. My specialist will verify that." I was trying to convince VicRoads to give me my licence back.

"Your case will be reviewed in due course. Until then, you mustn't drive."

"I'm *not* driving. I said that already. I wouldn't do that. But you have to listen to what my neurologist has to say about this."

"As I've told you, Mrs McAllister, your case will be reviewed in due course."

"That's it? I've been sitting here for almost an hour waiting to speak to someone, and when I do, you're not listening to me. I'm not saying, 'let me drive'. I'm asking when are you people even going to talk to my neurologist? 'In due course' could be any time."

"Unfortunately, that's all …"

"Don't 'unfortunately' me!" I slammed the phone down. The satisfaction from doing so was short-lived.

"A written off car, unfeeling bureaucrats, and a group of people who've turned their backs on me to appease a schizophrenic dope-fiend who thinks he's God. Every day I get up and try my best and that's what I get for my troubles?"

"Muuuuuwww." Sheba didn't think it was fair either.

"And pretty soon I won't even have someone to share a meal with."

"Muuuuuwww."

"Except you, of course." I gave her a stroke as she sauntered by.

I stood under the skylight. I had a Buddha on the mantelpiece. Would it really be so ridiculous to ask for help? It couldn't hurt. *Okay God, whatever you are, this is me. I got nothing. Here I am, I surrender.* Kneeling was not enough. I lay face down in front of the meditating Buddha, cried and prayed.

Later that afternoon, the phone rang.

"Anna, it's Helen." Helen was from the folk band. "I was ringing up to see how you are." She laughed nervously. "Of course, we haven't seen you at band practice lately, with everything that's gone on."

"You sure haven't. I wouldn't go near the place. I miss it though."

"Has anyone else been in touch with you?"

"Hmph." She took that as the 'no' it was intended to be.

"I see," she said. She didn't sound pleased. "It seems to me you've been dropped like a hot potato."

"Thank you. I have. It wouldn't be so bad if I had a car."

"Why? What's wrong with your car?"

"You haven't heard? I crashed it." I told her what had happened.

"Oh, Anna, that's terrible. It never rains but it pours."

"That's for sure. If I had a car, things would be so much easier. But I'm stuck here with my thoughts a lot of the time at the moment."

"Yes. I can well imagine. Let's have a coffee next time I come into Castlemaine."

"Sounds good."

"I'm annoyed nobody has even called you. It's like everyone's scared of Simon because of the way he is at the moment."

"Maybe they are," I said.

"Yes, well, Simon does have a history of this kind of thing you know."

"Does he?" It was the first I'd heard of it.

"Yes, he did this to me many years ago – accused me of being after him, trying to seduce him."

"You're kidding," I said, trying not to burst out laughing.

"About ten years ago."

"But you've been married to Gerry for twenty years. You'd never even look at another man."

"Yes, I have been, and no, I would never even think of another man," she said, amused.

"This is madness," I said.

"It is. When Simon goes into this other state of mind, reality is temporarily on hold. It happens to him every couple of years. He finds a vulnerable woman – and without wanting to offend you at all, Anna, you're vulnerable …"

"That's okay Helen, I'm not offended."

"He finds the most vulnerable woman in his circle, makes friends with her, then decides that she's after him, sapping his spiritual energy, or is the devil incarnate or whatever."

"Satan. That's what he said to me. It's because of all the dope he smokes, isn't it?"

"I would say so, Anna. If he stopped, he would be a lot more stable."

"Like that's ever going to happen."

"Exactly."

"So, he did this to you?"

"Yes. He came up to me in a bar one night, and in front of everyone started on about me having caused him much strife and disaster. Told me I was the Whore of Babylon."

I couldn't stop myself; I burst out laughing this time. "My God! What did you say?"

"I didn't get the chance to say anything. He turned on his heels and stormed off, leaving me to wonder what it was all about. Remember Jane Sanders? Same thing happened to her," Helen told me. "He really scared her. She changed her phone number and everything, almost moved back to Ballarat."

"Does he ever get violent when he's like this?"

"No, nothing like that, more defensive. He feels he's being attacked. Spiritually."

I groaned. That was the end of that 'friendship'. When would I ever stop attracting people into my life that took and gave nothing back? A few days later, another member of the band called. She wanted to know how I was going as well. Perhaps the prayer hadn't been irrational after all.

Not till You're Eighteen

It was finally happening. Finn was turning eighteen. He would no longer be my responsibility. I felt a mixture of pride, relief and dread. I'd spent the last eighteen years with a set plan. Now, here was the rest of my life in front of me. Finn was also looking ahead – to working, saving, being independent, being able to pay the rent; as well as cars, girls, parties and getting drunk legally.

It was also now his responsibility to vote, not drink and drive, not do drugs and generally keep his nose clean. I wasn't worried he couldn't, just that if he did happen to stuff up, the police would not be calling me in to smooth things over. It would all be on him. 'Cutting the apron strings' – the dilemma mothers have been facing since the dawn of time.

"We better talk about the party."

"You'll have to go and stay somewhere else for the weekend, Mum."

"Oh, will I now?" I hadn't thought of that. Fifty or more teenagers playing grunge metal and partying until sunrise? Of course I would. "This was a conversation we should have had before now," I said as I turned the TV off.

For a teenager, the eighteenth birthday party was a declaration to the world. He'd been thinking about this for months. "Of course you can't be here," he said as though it went without saying.

"Hmph. Kicked out of my own house. Astounding."

"It's my house too."

"Yes, true, but if the house gets trashed it's me who has to pay. And me who won't be able to find another house to rent because of an 'incident' on my tenancy record."

"It's not gonna happen, Mum," he said calmly.

"What, you psychic all of a sudden? Think that's part of turning eighteen too, do you?"

He made his *I'm annoyed* sound.

"I'm just saying you can't predict what's going to happen. Parties aren't what they were when I was your age. And even back then things happened."

"Do you mean you won't let me have my eighteenth party here?"

"No, of course not." How could I say that? "You can have it here. But we have to think very carefully about it. Who's coming? Who's going to keep an eye on people? And we need to tell the cops before the party happens, and the neighbours as well." I wasn't happy about it, but I said, "I'll stay at Carol's one night and Emma's the next. But I'm gonna do a drive-by just to put my mind at ease."

"You will NOT, Mum!"

After going off Sertraline, being seizure-free and having a protracted battle with VicRoads, I'd gotten my licence back and bought a cheap, fourth-hand car. It did the job. Most of the time.

"And who's going to stop me? Kicked out of my own house and not even allowed to check up every so often?"

"Muuum! You just said *one* drive-by. Now you're saying you're gonna do more than one?"

"If I want to." That annoyed him, but he knew he couldn't stop me. "Like I said, it's my name on the lease. If something gets broken, I'm the one who has to explain how it happened and pay for it ..."

He made another of those noises indicating primal frustration, but he knew it was true. Still, he tried to bargain for a reduction in the number of drive-bys.

"Just drive past once. And don't let anyone see you."

"Okay."

I'd do what I liked, but he didn't have to know that. "I could sneak past wearing a balaclava. Nobody would know it was me." He took the bait, just as I'd predicted.

"Yes they *would*, Mum!"

"Absolutely unbelievable." I dropped my bag down in Carol's lounge room. "Kicked out of my own house. Christ, I hope they don't do anything *really* stupid!"

"No, they'll probably be fine."

"Like you say – probably. Anything could happen."

"But if you were really worried you wouldn't have let him have a party, would you?"

"No, I guess not."

"He's a sensible lad."

"Nobody's sensible when they're pissed."

"True," she said laughing.

"We told the cops it was going to be happening. Angus and a couple of the others who look dangerous are going to keep an eye on things. And Finn too, of course. He better."

"He will. Most mothers wouldn't be as tolerant as you've been with Finn and his mates."

"Exactly. And now I'm about to pay."

"On the contrary, I think he respects the way you've treated him. I think his mates respect it too. They'll do their best to honour the fact that you've given them this much trust."

"Even when they're pissed?"

"Probably! Of course, the house will have to be cleaned up afterwards. But you're expecting that, aren't you?"

"Of course, and he's doing it *all*. Oh God!" I put my head in my hands the way I'd seen Mum do so many times. "How about I set up the couch and then go for a drive-by."

"Don't you think you should wait a couple of hours before you do that? It's not even dark yet."

"True. Let's go for a walk."

"Good idea," she said encouragingly.

*I*t had been dark about an hour. I couldn't wait any longer. There was a car behind us, so I couldn't drive slowly.

"I'll go around the block again to lose this car behind me. Can you see anything over there?"

"Just a few people on the footpath outside. The lights are on, a few cars. Nothing out of the ordinary."

I went around the block again and parked out of sight. Once the engine was off, the heavy metal was audible, along with the yelling and that whooping sound teenage girls make when they think something is funny. Angus, another new friend of Finn's, was standing on the front porch with one thumb in the pocket of his jeans, a can of beer in the other hand. He did look dangerous. He'd started weight training, had tattoos already and shaved his head. But I'd had some deep conversations with him and knew he was actually a pacifist. He just didn't look like one. There were some other people with him I'd never seen before. Of course they all had beers. But I didn't hear too much shouting. There were no explosions, gunshots or screams. Just crashes, whoops and heavy metal. So it seemed there was nothing to do but get back in the car and drive away.

"He's gonna cook me the most delicious dinner ever when I get home. I'm gonna make him!"

"Laugh about it."

"Ha."

*E*ach of his mates was pitching in with the clean-up, hangovers and all. It was a very laid back pace, but I allowed them that.

"I'm gonna go get a coffee down the street, leave you all to it."

"Aren't you gonna help?"

"Are you kidding? Your mess, you clean it up! You're doing very well though, *darling*," I said lovingly, putting my arm around his shoulder. Craig was grinning from ear to ear, no doubt relieved it was not his mum doing this to him in front of his mates. I wouldn't lift a finger until they had cleaned everywhere they'd been, attended to every bottle, dish and plastic plate.

As loud as I could, I called out, "Toodle-loo, darling!" hoping his mates would hear me say something so embarrassingly uncool.

They did an excellent job. When they'd finished, the house was tidier than usual.

"Don't forget to vote. And make sure you vote Labor," I said as he walked towards the front door.

"Yeah, sure, Mum," he said with the cheeky grin.

"I didn't mean that. Vote for who you think you should vote for, it's none of my business. I just couldn't resist!"

"I think I will vote Labor. Or the Greens. I haven't decided yet." This would be his first time voting. "Have a good time tonight," he said.

A whole lot of us were going to hear the Choir of Hard Knocks on election night. They were a group of homeless people who had been recruited for an ABC documentary. Sheba and I had watched every episode of the doco and heard them get better each week. The man who had recruited them, Jonathon Welch, had sought out people on the street who were sleeping rough, had been in jail or had no prospects of finding work. A group had been formed and taught to sing. The difference between the first episode and the last was phenomenal. Welch had said that there was no such thing as someone who could not sing, just talent waiting to be brought out. The choir had been touring Australia. Tonight it was Castlemaine's turn.

Castlemaine was a socially conscious town. We didn't have any fast food Mc-outlets, but welcomed groups like this with open arms and wallets. The Theatre Royal was packed. Halfway through the night the lights went up for interval. Someone came to the microphone.

"Ladies and gentlemen! Just thought you might like to know that the Howard government looks set to be thrown out of parliament. It seems Mr Howard himself has lost his seat." There was applause and cheers at this announcement. I looked around and saw a few with indignant expressions, but they were in a minority. John Howard had gone too far, and we had told him so.

Last Post

Uncle Jim had gone into aged care. We were spending Christmas Day with him.

"Put the brakes on, that's it," the nurse told me as we maneuvered him into position behind his walking frame. "Have a nice lunch, see you when you get back," she said as we walked slowly with him towards the exit door.

"How do we do this? Do you turn around with your back to the seat?"

"Uh-huh," he said, concentrating on not losing his balance. He got himself in position to sit in the passenger seat.

"Watch your head," I told him.

On arriving at our house, Finn got the walker out of the boot while I opened the car door. With one hand under each armpit, I pulled him up, imagining that would be enough for him to do the rest. Finn was ready and waiting with the walker, his arm holding the car door so it would not close. Uncle Jim stayed sitting in the car.

"Um … How do we do this? Turn and face that way a bit more maybe?" I said, pointing to the walker and Finn. Now push yourself up. Push, breathe, like you're having a baby … or maybe that's not the best analogy …" He laughed, but he still couldn't get out of the car.

"I guess we'll have to take our Christmas lunch to your place and have it there," Finn said, after we'd spent ten minutes trying to get him out.

"Looks that way," he replied.

When we arrived back at the hospital, a nurse opened the car door, reached around behind him and lifted him up unceremoniously by the belt hook of his trousers. He didn't have a choice then. He had to move. *One of the tricks of the trade,* I thought to myself. Christmas lunch was enjoyable, tasty and accompanied by background Christmas carols sung by Elvis Presley, and Dean Martin crooning 'I'm Dreaming of a White Christmas'. After about half an hour, we realised something else was not as it had once been. Uncle Jim didn't know who we were.

"Anna. And Finn, your great nephew."

It took another ten minutes to explain to him where we fitted in to his life, after which he simply continued eating his dessert, quite happy with the explanation. It would be our last Christmas together.

Three months later, we got a phone call from the hostel.

"Good morning. Could I please speak to Anna McAllister?"

"Yes?"

"Hello, this is Sandra from Castlemaine Hospital calling. I'm very sorry, but James McAllister passed away this morning at about two o'clock. I'm really, *really* sorry …"

I let out a cry which got Finn out of bed instantly.

"Anna, it's okay to call back later if that's what you need to do."

Finn entered the room. He was in my arms straight away, knowing it must have been either Uncle Jim or Sheba.

"Uncle Jim."

He hesitated and in a mature voice said, "Just hold on, Mum, I'll be back in a minute." I presumed it was to cry, but he wasn't about to tell me. When he came back out of his room, he showed no sign of it. We sat on the purple couch for a while in silence. I made us some tea and brought it to the coffee table.

"I'm gonna call Michael and tell him I'm not coming to work." Finn had secured himself some construction work with his mate Max's boss after refusing to go to school anymore.

Half an hour later, there was a knock at the door. Max and Michael had gone to the trouble of buying a condolence card. We stood around for a few minutes talking. Nothing seemed like the right thing to say. All that mattered was that they were there.

"Have the week off. Anything you need just call, okay?"

"Thanks," we both said. "Come to the funeral. That's something you can do," I said as I saw them out.

"'Course," said Max.

Closing the door after them, I felt myself going into denial as I realised I was the one who would be expected to organise it. Dad was having health issues, so I doubted he would be able to come or even help with the organisation. I would call and ask him to send us photos. My heart sank as I imagined the call.

"Let's do something normal and everyday, like have breakfast, yeah?"

"Good idea, Mum."

"We can finalise details tomorrow. Now, is there anyone who'd like to have a viewing?" asked the funeral director.

"I do."

"And start giving some thought to where you'd like people to get together afterwards. But that's all for today, I won't fill your head up with anything else."

"Oh well, it's all got to be done I suppose, I mean ... I *know* it's got to be done ... never done anything like this before, it's all an education, have to do it all properly for his sake ... he'd want some effort put in, I know I would ... I'm talking too much, aren't I?"

He smiled understandingly. What a job. Listening to people with verbal diarrhoea trying to block out the reason they were there in the first place.

There was just enough time to go to the supermarket before my appointment with the priest.

*F*ather Stephen Williams had taken me on as the gardener at the Anglican Church. I was not obliged to become a member of the congregation, which suited me fine. None of the parishioners had asked me if I wanted to know more about God. *And they better bloody not,* was my way of looking at things. My family, the blue-rinse set at my cousin's wedding, the church Linda went to that told her she couldn't have friends like me and Finn … If that was what Christianity did to you, I was not interested. It seemed to me that if you thought you were one of the 'chosen' ones, you must also think yourself better than everyone else.

Only thing was, Father Stephen didn't fit that mould. He didn't look down on anyone. Even the guy who had been caught in the vestry trying to steal candle holders got decent treatment from him. Instead of bawling him out and asking him what the hell he was doing there, apparently Father Stephen had simply walked in and asked, "Can I help you?"

"This rose bed is looking lovely now." He nodded towards the last job I'd done for him. The grass was in need of a mow before it got out of hand. As he walked me around showing me other jobs that would soon need doing, we talked about the funeral.

"Have you been able to contact all the people you wanted to?"

"Yes. Dad can't come, though. He's too sick. Mum was a nervous wreck at the mere thought of him travelling all this way."

"If you'd like me to give him a call, ask him if he feels the need to talk, I'd be more than happy to." I looked at him, astonished. He laughed at the expression on my face. "That goes for your mother as well, of course."

"That would be marvellous. I'll ask them."

"And have you thought about where you want people to have refreshments afterwards?"

"There's a hall opposite the cemetery. That's the best place, I think. Nothing too flash or expensive. Keep it simple. That's what he would have wanted."

Father Stephen smiled. "You're saying that he was a practical, frugal man? That fits in with other things you've told me about him."

"He was. He taught Finn how to be practical, think outside of the box, encouraged him to be himself, and now look at him. He's made some really good friends, and he's never been out of work. In this town where supposedly there is none. The Australian work ethic. He must have got that from Uncle Jim; he can't have got it from me …"

"Anna, you do say unfair things about yourself sometimes. How did this get done?" he asked me, gesturing to the rose bed. "When you were asleep?" A slight frown passed over his face. "And what do you think you've been doing these past eighteen years? Sitting in front of the television doodling on the newspaper?" he added with a questioning expression.

"Of course not. I've been working hard." I didn't know why I put myself down that way. "You're right. I've got this 'program' in my head that makes me say those kinds of things about myself sometimes."

"Well, you need to install a new program. Change the default setting."

"Yes, perhaps I should."

"*He* seems to know just what to say. He has this measured tone in his voice. When he talks … no …when he *listens* to you. It's like he's tuning into what you're saying and trying to imagine what you're feeling. Only he's not trying. He doesn't have to. He gets what you're saying." At dinner, Finn was listening as I tried to explain what it was about Father Stephen that impressed me so much. "Anyway, I reckon he's a pretty special person."

"You're not thinking of getting into God are you, Mum?" Finn asked, knowing what the answer would be.

"Oh, good grief, no."

"Did you go to the funeral parlour?" Finn asked.

"Yes. They said Uncle Jim would be ready tomorrow."

"What for?'

"A viewing."

Finn looked at me, frowning. "A *viewing?* You want to *see* him? Even though he's …" He cringed. "You're not expecting me to do that as well, are you? 'Cos I won't. No matter what you say, I will *not* look at him like that."

"You don't have to, luv. Nobody has to, and I'm not saying you should. It's just an option they give you."

"I'm glad you told me that, Mum," he said with relief in his voice.

"So that's just about everything done. The only other thing we have to do is go to the op-shop and get you a suit. We can do that tomorrow."

"No, I'll just wear that brown jacket and …"

"That's what you think." He wasn't going to a funeral in casual clothes, no matter how much times had changed.

I gasped. "Oh my God."

My son had just walked into the lounge room wearing the ten-dollar suit we'd bought him. He looked like a million bucks.

"You look *amazing*. Why haven't we bought you one before?"

"Dunno, Mum."

I walked around, admiring him from all angles. "*Wow!*"

"Yeah, okay. I get it, Mum … How do I do this?" He held up the tie they'd thrown in for nothing. I put it around the back of my neck.

"I used to do this every day."

"Yeah?" He found it hard to imagine.

"We wore ties at high school. You got in trouble if you didn't." He found that hard to imagine as well and sniggered. Except for the day he had worn the T-shirt with Fuck printed on it, he wore whatever he wanted.

"Around your neck, shorter on the left side, then put the right side over the left and under the …"

"Look it up on the internet."

"No! We can do it ourselves. We don't need …"

"Muuum! We've got to go soon, there's no time."

"Yeah, alright. One day they'll just take our brains out and attach us to these bloody things," I said gesturing to the computer. "Then we won't have to remember anything."

"Yeah, whatever …" he said as he typed in 'put on a tie' and clicked Enter.

"Today I'm going to teach you how to tie a Windsor knot." On the screen was a young man standing next to a mannequin. It was wearing a suit. Step by step he demonstrated. "First you find the right balance depending on the length of your tie." Finn followed along, and within a minute it was done.

I allowed myself one more adoring gaze before we walked out the door.

Everyone had taken a seat under the marquee that was set up in the cemetery. Finn sat in the front row, eyes to the ground. Carol, Ben, Lisa, Emma, Stella, Jenny, Greg and Lyn were gathered around him. I got up to read the eulogy. "First of all, let me say that his brother Douglas, my Dad, deeply regrets his inability to be here today. They didn't see much of each other, especially the last few years, but they were in communication over the phone and through me and Finn. So – James Victor McAllister …"

"Of all the people he ever spoke about, their mother Vivienne was the one he spoke of most highly. I wish I could have met her myself, but she died a long time before I was born. Anything I have ever heard about her confirms she was a compassionate, caring woman who never tired of making their home one of love, stability and goodness. His wife Lily was the same. I'm sure he's glad to see her again after all this time as well."

Finn had long eyelashes. I looked at them as he continued to sit with his head down. I felt tears coming, but thought instead about the time he had cut them shorter, their length being a source of extreme embarrassment. Women spent huge amounts of money to make their eyelashes look like his did. I had told him to stop cutting them, telling him they would grow back even longer. I didn't know if it was true, but it worked. He never cut them again. I got the lump in my throat under control and kept going.

When it was finished, I ended the eulogy by saying "Personally, I don't know how Finn's and my life would have turned out if I hadn't had his support and encouragement when we moved up here. Bringing Finn up in the country was something I felt strongly about, and Uncle Jim made it possible by helping us find accommodation, fixing things and being part of Finn's and my life. He will be sorely missed. God bless him, and may he rest in peace."

"I didn't know James McAllister. But I know Anna, and I have a great deal of respect for her," Father Stephen told the gathering.

Respect? For me? I thought. The family could have been supportive. But instead, Mum's side had made a point of reminding me how unseemly it was to have a single mother as a family member, all in the name of God. But here was a priest standing in front of a group of people telling them he respected me. The church stereotypes I'd collected in my mind started falling away like bark on a gum tree in a strong wind.

The funeral director's son played the 'Last Post'. The Australian flag on his coffin was replaced with the peace flag that Finn and I had made for him.

"We have entrusted James Victor McAllister to God's merciful keeping, and now we commit his body to be buried in the ground, earth to earth, ashes to ashes, dust to dust. In sure and certain hope of the resurrection to eternal life …"

His body was committed to the Earth and soil thrown over the coffin. Those of us who knew it said the prayer, "Our Father who art in Heaven, hallowed be Thy name, Thy Kingdom come, Thy will be done on Earth as it is in Heaven ..."

An older gentleman from the funeral parlour approached me with a flower from the wreath, presented it to me and bowed. It was the kind of thing men of that generation would do; same as taking off their hats inside, opening a door for someone, standing up when a woman entered the room. I imagined Uncle Jim doing the same thing.

"Thank you," I said to him.

He didn't say a word because he knew there was nothing worth saying. He nodded kindly and walked away.

The times they are a-changin', again

At their kitchen table, Mum and I ate toast and jam and drank tea made with the kettle I kept telling her to get rid of. Looking around the room, I noticed the latest piece of political opinion, a newspaper headline plastered onto a canister with sticky tape. It read 'Not Sorry'. This was in reference to the debate surrounding Australian Aborigines and the treatment they had received. An apology for the way they had been treated by the first white settlers was something John Howard had believed was unnecessary. Kevin Rudd, on the other hand, when he became prime minister, had made a point of apologising to the Australian Aborigines at the first sitting of parliament. Mum had been vocal about how 'reedeeculous' it was. I was proud my vote had contributed to it. Therefore, Mum and I disagreed, a very common theme with us.

"How can you say that? Exactly the same thing happened to you, can't you see?"

"Oh, goot grief, what a lot of nonsense," she said indignantly.

"Why? Because you had houses and cars and they hunted kangaroos?"

"Yes," she said as if I had defeated my own argument. "Zat iss one reason. There are many others." I cringed. I didn't want to hear the others.

"It's not about what you had and what they didn't. It's about having a home and then all of a sudden not having one, just because a bunch of power-mongers decided they wanted to take it over. That's *exactly* what happened to you!"

The debate had been sparked by a phone call to the program Mum was listening to while we ate breakfast. The 'shock-jock' whose program it was made it hard to digest the toast and jam.

"Mum, I know there's no point me saying anything to you about some things. But I'll never stop trying."

"Zen I will zhusst haff to grin and bear it I suppose. Another cup of tea? From ze rusty kettle?"

I handed her my cup. "By the way Mum, I'm thinking of starting to go to church." Turning from the kitchen sink, she stopped in her tracks, a look on her face that said she didn't believe it but wished she could.

"Goot. I'm very glad to hear it, Anna." She smiled as she put the kettle on the stove. "About time," she added. I rolled my eyes.

Dad spent his Sunday mornings in bed reading the newspaper. I had started making a point of talking to him by himself. This morning I had a copy of the order of service from Uncle Jim's funeral to give him. I told him as much about the service as I could possibly remember. When I'd exhausted that avenue of conversation, I started telling him about the latest gardening job I'd done. "I love getting my hands in the dirt, pulling out weeds, pruning or planting something. Then stepping back, looking at it and saying, 'I did that'."

"That's good, luv. Being out in the fresh air is healthier than being stuck inside all day."

"Sure is. There's something else I've been thinking of taking up. But I'm still trying to decide. I'm thinking I might start going to church." It made me uncomfortable saying it. As far as I knew, Dad wasn't a big fan.

"That's good, luv. It's good to have faith."

"I had no idea! All these years and you never said a word." That was Dad; never one to make a fuss about anything. "You believe in God?"

"Yes, I pray every night." He said it as if I'd asked him how many sugars he wanted in his tea.

I was starting to see that I was more like him than I realised. I'd left home as soon as I could find somewhere. But it wasn't him I'd been walking away from. It was because I had to. I hadn't *wanted* to leave either of them with so much unresolved business. It wouldn't be long till I found out how Mum and Dad had felt while watching me getting into the taxi all those years ago.

You can't stop your kids from leaving home. It's what they're supposed to do. Sometimes there's even an element of 'for God's sake do it' involved, no matter how much you love them. After all the hours of lost sleep wondering where they are and when they'll be back … the parties they go to … the things they get up to that they won't tell you about until decades later when it no longer matters … the arguments that start happening as your hormones are declining and theirs are surging ….

"I've found somewhere to live, Mum," Finn told me as he came into our kitchen.

In an instant, all that rationalizing ceased to mean anything. He'd be expecting that. The tears were not from the onions I had been chopping. He came over and held me in his arms.

"Where?" I asked, wiping the tears away with the back of my hand so as not to get onion in them.

"A share house in Taylor Street."

"When?"

"Next week."

"What the …" I turned from the sink, my hands still wet and hanging by my side. Eighteen years, and then, all of a sudden, a week left.

"It's not like we're never gonna see each other again, Mum."

"I know. I know. It's just …" I looked at his fresh, young face. The face I had looked at adoringly while he slept in the baby carrier, the face that looked adoringly at Sheba as he patted her, the face that lit up when he got his first bicycle, the face that contorted with pain when he hurt himself. The face I looked at every day.

"Hello, Blossom," announced Father Stephen in his usual cheerful manner.

"G'day." I looked up unenthusiastically from the iris bed.

He raised one eyebrow to indicate his awareness that something was wrong. "What's the matter? It can't be that bad, surely?"

"Yes it can. My son left home yesterday."

"Ah," he replied. "That's a very significant event – very significant indeed."

"Sure is," I answered. "It's good, it's the way it's meant to be. And he's only on the other side of town. It's just left me feeling ... a bit flat. Look, about the gardening this morning; I keep stopping and staring into space. So I'll only be charging half price 'cos I'm only half here."

He laughed and said, "Don't worry about that. It's perfectly understandable you're feeling low this morning. The Eucharist service is starting soon. Come in if you feel so inclined, and we can say a prayer for this new stage in his life. And yours."

"That sounds like a good idea," I replied, then hesitated. "But I might cry in front of everyone. They don't know me. Why should they have to sit there waiting for me to get it together?"

"Nonsense!" he exclaimed with a dismissive gesture. "This is a very understanding parish. Besides, most of them have been through the same thing, some of them six or seven times."

"But," I told him as we walked towards the church, "if I see any light or Jesus in front of me, I'm going straight to Bendigo."

"What's in Bendigo?"

"The mental hospital."

He threw his head back and laughed. "Come on, time for a spot of religion!" he said in an exaggerated English accent as he linked arms with me.

You can be religious and have a sense of humour at the same time? That's a new one on me .... There was that 'strong wind' again, stripping yet more pieces of bark from off of that gum tree. It couldn't hurt to see what these people were like.

"Found this one in the garden," Father Stephen announced. The others in the chapel to the side of the church looked around, murmured greetings and smiled in welcome. Someone handed me his prayer book open at the right page and went to get another one for himself.

As Father Stephen moved to his chair, he pointed to the book in my hand and said, "You'll catch on," then said, "The Lord be with you."

"And also with you," said everyone except me. A petite elderly woman and I made eye contact. We smiled at each other.

There had been a woman named Julianne. I'd first met her when we were in the same community singing group. She had become very ill and was housebound towards the end of her life. Father Stephen and I were in his garden talking about her upcoming funeral.

"I don't suppose you'd like to participate in Julianne's service, would you?" He laughed at my eyebrows, which had suddenly shot up as far as they could go. What did he imagine I could do?

"Me? What do you mean?"

"The traditional part of church was something she valued. In her will she specified all the trappings – choir, incense, prayers, psalms, the lot. I'm looking for two people to carry candles in front of her coffin as she's being led out to the hearse. Is that something you'd like to do by any chance?"

I stared at him. The subtle smile on his face was one of amusement.

"Um ... It's just not something I've ever been asked to do. I mean, I'm not even part of the church ..."

"I'm a great believer in getting everyone involved. The more hands on deck the better. So have a think about it and let me know by Thursday, okay?"

I liked the idea. "No, I don't need to think about it. I'd love to."

And so it was that on the day of her funeral I was handed a long white robe to put on, a religious garment. There was a silent, but no less intense, conflict going on inside me, a war of words.

What on earth am I doing? said one of the 'voices' in my head.

Something pretty special, something marvellous, said another.

I couldn't see it.

Religion is crap. Church hurts people. You were mad to say yes to this.

A bit late for that now, isn't it? You're doing this because Julianne loved ceremony. You're doing it for her. Get a move on.

I would do it because of her and not for any other reason.

There go those bells you like so much ... Ever wondered what it is about them? Hmm?

I saw Father Stephen out of the corner of my eye ushering me to join the others gathered outside. The service was about to begin.

Magnificent organ music filled the church as we processed up the aisle. Father Stephen followed the procession of cross and candle bearers, choir, and a man swinging an incense holder. Ornate stained-glass windows adorned the building on all sides. Incense filled the air – the most sublime I'd ever smelt. The church was packed to standing room only.

At the end of the service, Father Stephen signalled with a slight nod to me and the other woman whose help he had enlisted to be a candle bearer. It was time for us to take our places, ready to lead Julianne on her last journey anywhere. The candles were sitting in wooden holders on either side of the lectern. The organ started up, the choir started singing again in glorious harmonies. We turned towards the congregation in readiness to move. From the corner of my eye I saw the coffin being lifted and Father Stephen giving us another subtle nod. We set off slowly as we'd been instructed.

She deserved this, to be accompanied out with dignity. For the first time I understood that this really did matter. Not why, just that it did, and I was part of it. A woman I'd recently met stood at the back of the church. She was looking straight at me. I saw her face drop. We had shared our views on religion and had found they were the same. It was like I'd betrayed her. Only I hadn't. I knew straight away from the look on her face, so obviously disappointed, that her opinion of me had changed and would not change back. But I also felt something inside me that was like coming home.

No. No way known. What home?

Face it. You like this!

Shut the hell up. I'm trying to do something important here. Leave me alone.

I gulped and looked straight ahead, making sure there was no expression on my face that might betray the conflict going on inside me.

You're doing very well at this! And you want to do more of the same kind of thing, don't you?

Yeah, I do, okay? I do. Happy now?

Very.

Finn had just told me about the night he'd been walking home from a party. He had been in the bush, and had sat down in the middle of a bush track and started crying about Uncle Jim.

"Sounds like you got it all out of your system."

"It was weird. It just happened all of a sudden," he said. "I sat there for ages. I felt so much better when I finished."

"Excellent. Nothing wrong with crying."

"Being out in the bush must have reminded me of all the times we went camping."

I watched him drink his coffee. He'd gotten some tattoos and planned on getting more. He had a job, so he could afford them. His eyes were bright, there was colour in his cheeks. It seemed that his new-found freedom was not wearing him out. He was looking around the house. It wasn't that long since he had left, but he said, "It was cool how you let us have parties here, Mum. Lots of my friends have said that too."

"Good. I'm glad to hear it. I figured it was better to have you all here where I knew you'd be okay. And your mates were always really nice and never rude to me or anything. You might find this hard to believe, but I miss it."

"You'll have to make your own fun now. Throw some parties of your own, have people over for dinner."

"You're right. But I wonder if I need a three-bedroom place to do it in. The house is too big now."

"You thinking of moving?"

"Yeah. I think now might be good …." The timing was right. I had recently been told the unblinking speed woman, our landlady, wanted to cash in on her investment, she was thinking of selling up.

"There's a special way you have to open the front door," I told the estate agent. "You kind of have to lift the door and *then* twist to unlock it," I said, as I handed her the key which had a bend in it. I felt like a mother explaining her child's eccentricities to the kindergarten teacher.

"The door must have sunk. It happens with old houses," she told me.

"When we first moved in, I never used to lock anything: the house, the car … but that was a long time ago now …"

"Yes it was, wasn't it? Speaking of that, we couldn't find a copy of your original lease," she said.

"We didn't have one when we first moved here – not an official lease like the one we had with you."

"How long ago was that?"

"Fifteen years."

Epilogue

Remember at the beginning of the book I told you Finn was going to ask Natalie to marry him? She said yes.

I have a Tullamarine flight information website open on the internet, tracking their progress as I write this. They're two-thirds of the way to Laos and will land at approximately ten tonight our time. After Laos they will head to Vietnam, then Cambodia and home again 'to begin their life together', as they say. Of course, they began their life together ages ago. Perhaps now it's more to do with making babies. I haven't dared ask, not wanting to be the interfering mother-in-law.

When Finn left home, I wondered what I was going to do with the rest of my life. After having been a mother, anything else seemed to pale into insignificance. Longevity runs in both sides of my family, so I knew I had to make some decisions about my future. The first thing I decided is that Castlemaine is where I belong.

I divide my time between being an active member of the Anglican Church, working in other people's gardens, photography, writing and working in my own garden. Father Stephen retired a few years ago. My gratitude to him is beyond words. At first, some of my friends were worried when I started going to church regularly. But they have since breathed sighs of relief. It's now clear to everyone that what the church has done for me has nothing to do with being 'saved', and that I have no intention of trying to 'save' anyone else.

As well as finding a lovely girl to marry, Finn has landed himself a job in one of the many cafes in town. I look at his life and compare it to mine, especially when he was younger. He is not clueless like I was back then. I made a point of not sheltering him the way I had been sheltered.

It would have been easier to bring him up with a man around, there is no doubt about that. But that was not what was destined to happen. We were a single-parent family and we made it work. If this book can make a positive difference to the way society sees single-parent families, then I will have done what I set out to do.

The other thing that inspired me to write this book was that after moving hither and thither, we finally found stable accommodation. Not all single-parent families have this. It is absolutely ESSENTIAL. I'm extremely grateful to Emma for suggesting Finn and I take over the lease and the 'unblinking speed woman' for not kicking us out when she bought the place. Whoever you are, I am sure you were not on speed!

I hope you've enjoyed our story. The happily-ever-after ending is just the beginning. It's the end of the book, so I don't care how kitsch that sounds. What's that? Some of us always have to have the last word, don't they? She always says the same thing! She's getting old for a cat but she's still here. What did you say?

"Muuuuuwww."

It must be dinner time.

Credits

Gerry Rafferty, 'Baker Street', 1973
Foo Fighters, 'Baker Street' (cover), 1997
Black Sabbath, *Paranoid*, 1970
The Age, June, 2007
Stuart R Kaplan, *Tarot Classic*, US Games Systems, 1972

www.ingramcontent.com/pod-product-compliance
Lightning Source LLC
Chambersburg PA
CBHW030255010526
44107CB00053B/1723